# AM
# STRONG

the life and journey of an autistic pastor

Lamar Hardwick

eLectio Publishing

Little Elm, TX

www.eLectioPublishing.com

*I Am Strong: The Life and Journey of an Autistic Pastor*
By Lamar Hardwick

Copyright 2017 by Lamar Hardwick. All rights reserved.
Cover Design by eLectio Publishing.

ISBN-13: 978-1-63213-334-2
Published by eLectio Publishing, LLC
Little Elm, Texas
http://www.eLectioPublishing.com

Printed in the United States of America

5 4 3 2 1 eLP 21 20 19 18 17

The eLectio Publishing creative team is comprised of: Kaitlyn Campbell, Emily Certain, Lori Draft, Court Dudek, Jim Eccles, Sheldon James, and Christine LePorte.

**Publisher's Note**
The publisher does not have any control over and does not assume any responsibility for author or third-party websites or their content.

# CONTENTS

# FOREWORD

*The popular image of autism is with children. With that we must understand that children with autism will become adults with autism and we must be ready for them. Autism and other disabilities don't just stop in childhood.*

Growing up on the autism spectrum was often a challenge but today as an adult on the spectrum I'm so grateful to have overcome many obstacles thanks to my greatest champions in my life, my parents, family and therapists to have the opportunity to write several books today along with this foreword for Lamar's book. I have to say it's truly an honor.

Now, when I consult for parents it's usually when a child is just diagnosed but what happens when adults are the ones who are being diagnosed? What supports do we have out there to help them thrive? I share my personal experiences of growing up on the spectrum in the hopes I can educate and impact the lives of those in our community.

With this I introduce you to my dear friend Lamar Hardwick. In full-disclosure when Lamar asked for my help with his book I was overwhelmed with gratitude because in many ways I look at Lamar as a role model. Before Lamar shared his story I simply didn't think about adults diagnosed with autism. We live in a community where the emphasis is on early intervention and children with autism, so many times adults don't get the acknowledgement they deserve.

One of the talks I constantly give is the transition to adulthood for those with autism and other disabilities. The issue of what it is like to have your initial diagnosis when you are an adult was not on my radar screen.

A saying we have is if you've met one individual with autism you've met just that one individual with autism. While I was diagnosed on the autism spectrum at the age of four, Lamar wasn't diagnosed till the age of 36.

Lamar's and my story vary immensely compared to other stories you are going to hear today of other autistics, but what strikes me is the similarities between us.

We need to help those with autism get a diagnosis as early as possible. Early intervention is the key to help our loved ones across the lifespan regardless of autism or another special need. One way we can do this is about teaching people about the early signs of autism. As we share more about things like those signs we need to make sure that adults also can receive a proper diagnosis like Lamar. No one should fall through the cracks.

This question of falling through the cracks becomes important because a common but often unspoken question for special needs families is "what will happen to my child when I'm gone?" This question can bring a great deal of anxiety and uncertainty. Add on an autism diagnosis and it can feel even more overwhelming.

I was completely nonverbal until I was two and a half years old and didn't start saying my first few words until I was three. I wouldn't start speaking in complete sentences until I was five. Along the way I'd also have challenges with expressive and receptive language disorder, severe sensory integration dysfunction, auditory processing disorder, twirling, dysgraphia (a handwriting disorder), motor challenges, anxiety and emotional issues due to my lack of speech.

Like Lamar, I felt different. I felt like I wasn't enough. I was bullied constantly growing up and didn't have one friend until high school. For so long I saw my story as a constant challenge and when being told by my parents about having autism at eleven and a half years old, being mad about my diagnosis. I'd fight with myself all the time, confused and scared. I'd ask God before I would go to bed saying things such as...

"Why me?"

And "Why would someone do this to me?"

Thankfully my thought process changed from seeing autism as a hindrance to finding out that autism was one of my greatest strengths in my life. It wasn't easy but thanks to physical, occupational, speech, music, and theater therapy along with a large amount of visual schedules, reward systems in the household and in school and having a 'village' of supports in my families unconditional love of me, like Lamar, I've been able to overcome many of my challenges. My faith has been something that has been restored to this day.

While transitioning to adulthood I was able to be varsity captain of our high school basketball team, lead in my school play, student council president and, for one of my first dreams ever, getting accepted into college, was able to get into all 15 colleges I applied too. I would later graduate from college, write several best-selling books, become a disability advocate and anti-bullying activist and travel the country as an international motivational speaker who would speak at hundreds of venues a year.

One of the reasons I became even more curious about religion & autism was when I was the autism film consultant for the 2012 hit Joyful Noise starring Queen Latifah and Dolly Parton. The film is a gospel choir dramedy about two strong-minded women who are forced to work together to save a small town gospel choir after budget cuts threaten to shut them down. One of the characters in the film, Queen Latifah's characters son was a teenager with Asperger Syndrome. I was brought on to make sure that this portrayal was as realistic to autism as possible.

During my role on the film I became more experienced on some of these topics and later when giving talks would often be asked about the topic of religion & autism.

I consider one of my biggest role models in our autism community to be John Elder Robison who wrote the book Look Me in the Eye in 2005 which quickly become a NY Times Best-Seller. John, like me and Lamar, was diagnosed with autism. John's story has helped pave the way for others such as me and Lamar to share our stories. I can only hope that by Lamar's story being shared here that we can inspire more people with autism to do the same.

Like Lamar, there are countless people out there who have felt weak and felt like they weren't enough. But, as a community we are strong.

**Lamar is strong.**

His ability to never give up, to work on his social skills, and become a pastor has made him a role model to countless today. Whenever I speak I often share Lamar's story. We may be different than others but like one of the leading autism advocates in the world Dr. Temple Grandin says, "Different not less."

Dr. Grandin's quote inspired me later to come up with my own quote that I shared with my college peers when I came out about having autism to the first time when I shared with them that, "Autism can't define me, I define autism."

Lamar's story is a testament of how great things truly are possible for people in our community. His faith is something we should all aspire to. Regardless if it is in religion or just in what we are passionate about in our careers and in the successes of our loved ones. While going to a catholic university in Seton Hall University I learned about the importance of serving others like Lamar shares in that book. I hope you will be able to serve others in your communities after hearing about Lamar's story.

With that thought, I hope his book will help you explore how broad the autism spectrum actually is. So many people come up to me today and say, "You have autism? I would have never known." I'm sure Lamar has heard the same. We sometimes are considered to have "invisible disabilities." Each one of us though deals with challenges that others may never be aware of so please remember to be kind to everyone you meet.

This couldn't be any truer then accommodating those with autism and other special needs in churches, synagogues, congregations and many more places of worship. There have been places around the country hosting disability-friendly worship services. Other organizations have provided guides to help children with special needs with visual schedules to better understand the church and even religion. This has been something I've been very proud to take part in.

While you read his story I hope you will take away a few of his lessons to help better your own journey in what you are doing today. I know I have. But above all else I hope that you will learn that you should always have faith in your loved ones.

**Autism doesn't come with an instruction guide. It comes with a family who will never up.**

**Faith is one and the same. Never lose faith.**

*"Let all that you do be done in love." – 1 Corinthians 16:14*

Kerry Magro

International award-winning speaker
Best-selling author of
*Defining Autism From The Heart and Autism* and *Falling in Love*

# CHAPTER 1
# I AM MISSING

## Missing Memories

"Don't let the excitement of youth cause you to forget your creator. Honor him in your youth before you grow old and say, 'Life is not pleasant anymore.'"[1] I'm not perfect, and I don't even pretend to be, but for the most part, I try to do what's right. I particularly try to do what the Bible says. Mostly because I'm a Christian, but also because I try to be a good example to my children and to my church because I am a pastor.

The Bible tells me I should be doing a lot of things that I struggle with doing. Sometimes I am not nearly as generous, compassionate, or gracious as I should be, but I try. I honestly try. This verse, though, is one of those parts of the Bible I totally nailed. I can honestly say that when Solomon advises not to get caught up in the excitement of my youth, I didn't, and it wasn't because I was really trying all that hard. Heck, I never even read this verse when I was considered a "youth." The reason I absolutely nailed the application of this verse is because my childhood wasn't all that exciting.

I don't remember much about my early childhood. I suspect that is because for the most part, my childhood was uneventful. I don't have grand memories of birthday parties with friends or spending the day at an amusement park with family. I struggle to recall the names of my grade school teachers, and it is almost impossible to recall any names of childhood friends. Childhood was less than a series of moments, and my childhood was a desperate search for significance in a rapidly changing world of social hyperactivity. With that being said, there were at least two critical factors that shaped my identity growing up.

---

[1]Ecclesiastes 12:1 NLT.

1

## Military Life

My father was in the military. Life as a military "brat" is a unique experience that normally only other "brats" can identify with. When you are young, it is extremely difficult to understand the weight of being the child of a service member. Don't get me wrong—there were a lot of advantages to having a father in the military. By the time I was ten years old, my family and I had traveled to many places in Europe. The memories are faint, but I do recall our time spent living in Bad Kreuznach, Germany. We even had the privilege of visiting Holland and Austria during our time spent overseas. Those years spent living outside of the United States helped shape my young and impressionable mind.

The thing I remember most about our time spent in Europe is the food. The food was always good. Like many children, I had my favorite places to eat and favorite places to visit, but my favorite among those places was a little candy shop that sat on the corner of a busy intersection just a few blocks away from our home. This place was magical. It was like a scene straight out of *Charlie and the Chocolate Factory*. The colors were vast, the space was quaint, and the chocolate was absolutely to die for. Gathering at the local candy shop on the weekend was a staple in my life in a distant land with a different language. No matter how different I was from all of the other military kids, and no matter how different I was from my German neighbors, the one thing that made me just like everyone else was the candy store. At the candy store, true community was present. Everyone was equal, and everyone was accepted, and although I can recall the beginning stages of discerning that I was different than the other kids, the candy store helped level the playing field.

Growing up in a different country with a different language, different customs, and a different culture actually did a lot to hide my differences. At the same time, it helped me to grow an appreciation for how different everyone in the world was. One of the primary reasons I love and champion the cause of cultural diversity is that I spent my early years immersed in diversity.

2

The major challenge facing many military children is the lack of stability. As a child, I can remember moving, a lot. Approximately every three years, my father was reassigned to a new military base. I was born in Killeen, Texas, but that is all I know. We moved sometime after my birth and well before my memory of having lived there. My life began as a mystery, and for the most part, the mystery continued on into my early adult years.

In many ways, the mystery was due to constantly being a moving target. Moving from place to place is probably the factor most responsible for masking the more serious issues I faced as a child. Of all the memories I have of childhood, friendships are strangely vague and in some cases nonexistent.

Growing up and never being able to establish roots meant I had difficulties establishing relationships. Every three years, we were given a reset button to press, and we began the process of creating new memories. The problem is that I have no memories of all the "others," or at least not like most people. My life was a mystery with very few clues as to how to figure myself out.

## Pastor's Kid

The second critical factor that shaped my identity was that my father was also a minister. This meant that not only did I grow up a military brat, but I also grew up a PK (preacher's kid). I don't recall much about my father becoming a preacher. Prior to being shipped off to Germany, we lived for a few years at a military base in Georgia. I can recall attending church periodically. I even have some memory of attending two different churches. I later found out that each church only met twice a month on alternating weeks, which explained why we attended two different churches. Both were rural churches, tucked away somewhere on a country road that I couldn't find today if I were asked. What I cannot recall, however, is exactly when my father became a preacher.

Church was also a mystery. There is an entire section of our spiritual development as children that I am unaware of. I can't recall the names of the churches we attended. I can't recall the names of the pastors or the names and faces of any of the people. I have no recollection of Sunday school teachers or choir directors. My only memory is of my father being the pastor of a small little church we attended while being stationed in Germany.

The only vivid memory I have of church as a child is having my hand retracted from the communion plate that was passing across my lap. I can remember the warm summer day, mostly because the suit my mother made me wear was hot and itchy. It was uncomfortable, and it drove me crazy. In those days, I didn't like wearing certain fabrics. Something about certain textures irritated me—it was not just about what it did to my skin but mostly about what it did to me mentally. Of course, when you're a child, you wear whatever your parents pick out for you. Perhaps one of the only reasons I have a memory of church at all is that I can remember how I felt about having to wear the itchy, irritating suit and feeling completely isolated at the same time.

The plate passed across me from my right. In the plate were little crackers, which I later learned were communion wafers. I reached out to grab one, just as I had seen everyone else prior to me do, and just as my little hand reached out toward the plate, I felt a cold, gloved hand grip my wrist and pull my hand back away from the plate. I watched as the plate hovered across me just slightly in my line of sight and then moved into the hands of the person sitting on the other side of my mother. I watched my mother take a cracker, and the person next to her take one. As for me, I was apparently prohibited from doing the same.

I never quite understood what was happening in that moment. When I grew older and became a pastor myself, I realized that I had observed the church engaging in the Christian practice of communion. I understand that now, but what I remember is how I was made to feel at the time. I felt different. I felt singled out, isolated, and disconnected. This was a rather normal occurrence for me outside of the church. The lack of memories about friendships and fun as a child is the result of not having friends to create

4

memories with. When I felt isolated that day in church, it seemed to only confirm what I already knew about myself. I was different. I was an outsider. I was a mystery that no one could figure out, and because I was so different and so deficient in my ability to relate well to others socially, it demanded that I be excluded from all attempts to build relationships with others, even God.

The combination of being a military brat and a preacher's kid was a deadly cocktail of confusion that led to me creating the false image I would learn to live with. Growing up in an environment where my father's service to country and God was all I knew, it forced me to embrace the idea that life was about giving yourself to something greater than yourself, even at the cost of giving until the real you is completely gone.

As a young child, I had to figure out who I was on my own. Since one of my earliest and most vivid memories of church was one of isolation and rejection, I subconsciously came to believe that God must be disappointed in who I was and what I wasn't. I wasn't good enough to receive anything from his table, so faith, love, and hope became concepts that had no value to me because I believed I had no value to God. I was different, and even God didn't think I was worth his time.

## More than Me

Despite not having many memories, I do recall having a tremendous struggle with social interactions. I was born in 1978, and we didn't really know much about autism then. It just wasn't a word that came up too often. After all, I could talk. I often didn't talk, but I could. In those days, we just labeled it "shy," a label I would learn had several other derogatory labels attached to it. This made being a part of a big family a big deal for me.

Life in our home was interesting. I don't recall any one person in my family being a "social butterfly" except for my mother. My mother was the talker. She could talk to anyone about anything for any length of time. I never did understand how she could be so friendly. I actually thought it wasn't normal. She was almost superhuman in my eyes. I certainly didn't have whatever it was that gave her the courage to be so outgoing, and that was an early source of self-doubt for me as a child.

There weren't a lot of meaningful conversations in our home. Our home was almost always a very quiet and serene place. Of course, growing up as I did, I never quite understood that everyone's home did not operate in the same manner as my own, so I believed that everyone grew up not talking to their family members. It seemed natural to me because I preferred silence. Silence was good. In fact, I could go an entire day without talking to anyone, not because I did not have the ability to speak, but because I had little desire to.

Some of my silence was due to the style of parenting my parents subscribed to. In all honesty, I'm sure it was the same way they were reared. Children were not meant to make a lot of noise and a lot of fuss, and certainly children were not meant to have a voice in the family, at least not one that mattered. Truth is, for my early developmental years, that suited me just fine. I spent the majority of my time thinking and living inside of my own head.

As long as I can remember, I enjoyed reading. I am still an avid reader, and on most occasions, I will choose a good book over a great conversation. When I was young, I used to read myself to sleep nearly every night. My mother would have to come in and take the books off of my face because I would literally fight sleep to read, and of course I would eventually lose.

Books were a lot easier than people. People were scary and confusing. Books provided a space for me to learn and to live. In many ways, books became the doorway to the world for me. Almost everything I knew about people came from books. I am still a book learner. When I sense there is more information available that may impact or increase my abilities, I look for books, not people. I like people, and I enjoy the company of small groups of people in small doses, but books would win a head-to-head contest with people every time, hands down.

This worked well for a while, particularly in my early years. My love for books actually made me a good student. I made excellent grades in elementary school. While living in Germany, I was even placed in the talented and gifted program because of my intellect. Learning to read was the greatest thing I had ever accomplished. It helped me academically, but the real reason reading was such a joy was that it meant I could avoid having to converse with others. Books became my sanctuary; after all, God did not want me in his, so I had to find my own place of peace.

As long as I was home, everything was good. Reading worked. Solitude worked. Unfortunately, I couldn't live in my own world twenty-four hours a day, seven days a week. I had to go to school, and going to school meant I had to brave the noise and activity, and I had to socialize with other kids. I didn't like it at all. It was the worst part of being a kid.

Living in a relatively quiet home, living with my nose inside of a book, and having no internal desire or skills to socialize with other children created difficulties for me in school. On the surface, I seemed to do fine in how I related to the other children, but beneath the surface, I struggled to understand why I always seemed to live in a world where everyone seemed to know something I didn't. It was almost like the world was moving so much faster than I could make sense of it, and the result was that I was socially slower than most of my peers.

The problem was that there were no books for me to read that could possibly help me understand my peers, and it seemed that I was such a mysterious and odd little boy that I was equally as impossible to understand. That made me both frustrated and frightened. I was different, and for most of my peers, different meant deficient.

It was around this time, perhaps around fourth or fifth grade, that I would soon begin to discover that the world was much bigger than I had anticipated. The world I was thrust into was different than my world of books and silence; this world was more than me. It was more than the me that I was most naturally. The world was big, loud, and active, but I was small, quiet, and reserved. The world I was invited to be a part of was so dramatically different than the real me that it felt like it was just too big. "More than me" is a way I would describe it to myself. The world is more than me. Eventually, I would learn that the only way to have a fighting chance of surviving in this world that was *more* than me was to learn to be more than *me*. In other words, my survival was dependent on learning how to be someone I wasn't.

Middle school can resemble a jungle of wild, untamed animals that, given the right opportunity, will devour each other for the mere sake of establishing dominance. At least that was what it felt like to me when I was thirteen years old. Middle school is sometimes an experience that many kids try to wish away, but for me, it was an experience that made me wish myself away.

If I knew then what I know now, I would not only say that I was obviously autistic, I would also say that I was probably severely depressed because I didn't know what was wrong with me. I didn't want to be around anyone, and I didn't want to be around period. I didn't know what suicide was at that age, so I don't think that was ever an option, but what I did desperately want to do was to disappear, and for the most part, I did go away. In middle school, the social pressure of being the "shy" guy finally became so heavy that I disappeared. The real me disappeared into the abyss of depression and anxiety, and it would be nearly three decades before he would be rescued.

## I Am Missing

I have always been a fan of modern technology. I love gadgets. I suppose my love for gadgets and devices is similar to my love for books. Technology offers the opportunity to enter into a world completely void of the vicious voices that often violently abuse the meekest and the weakest in society. I love that recent technological advances have also made it easier for me to learn. I love that I can access written information at the click of a button. The Internet is a dream to someone like me who loves to lose himself in literature. I'm beginning to embrace e-books; however, I still love the smell and texture of a newly printed hardback book. Even so, there are times when I leverage technology to access new reading material quickly in order to satisfy my need for solitude.

The invention and advancement of mobile phones and tablets has changed the world by changing the way we communicate. Most mobile phone owners have the capability of connecting themselves to the world with the simple touch of a finger. There are many cases in which the improper use and abuse of these technological advances has caused harm to others, yet there are also many cases in which these advancements have been used to communicate and connect people across the globe for the common good.

One of the most significant uses of modern technology happened in 2013. In January of 2013, mobile devices were enabled with the capacity to receive Amber Alerts via text message or mobile phone applications. Within a matter of minutes, millions of wireless customers can receive alerts about missing children right on their mobile device. Messages about missing children go out to millions of people, instantly connecting them together as a concerned community committed to finding lost children.

One of the central themes in the Christian faith and tradition is finding the lost. The Bible is full of imagery, symbolism, and metaphors about God's concern to find those who are lost. Christianity, in a sense, has a fixation on lost things, and while that is essential to the practice of Christian faith, I'm afraid we have possibly lost something far greater in our quest for the "lost" — perhaps we are the ones who have gone missing.

The master storyteller Jesus gives us insight into the heart of the matter when it comes to lost things and lost people. One of the best places in the Bible to catch a glimpse of God's insight into the lost is the gospel of Luke. Chapter 15 records three stories that deal with "lost" things. This series of stories begins with a story about a lost sheep.

Imagine Jesus, surrounded by "lost" people, telling a story about what it feels like to be missing. His audience, Luke records, is some of what could be considered the worst offenders of their era. Sinners and tax collectors are present and accounted for. Also among the audience that day was the group known as the Pharisees. These guys normally have a pretty bad reputation among modern evangelical Christians, but perhaps they were not always as bad as we make them out to be. They didn't always agree with Jesus about the company he kept, so Luke records that he told them this story as a way of explaining his mission.

> "Which one of you, having a hundred sheep and losing one of them, does not leave the ninety-nine in the wilderness and go after the one that is lost until he finds it? When he has found it, he lays it on his shoulders and rejoices. And when he comes home, he calls together his friends and neighbors, saying to them, "Rejoice with me, for I have found my sheep that was lost." [2]

For years, I assumed that the primary point of this story is the sinfulness of the missing sheep. After all, the owner has to search for the little sheep that has gone missing. In many ways, this implies that the sheep is wrong or sinful. At the very least, the sheep is so different from the others that it seeks isolation.

The problem with this interpretation is that it may be the extreme opposite of the message Jesus intended to convey. "The problem is that many of us today hear 'sinner' and think only in religious categories." [3] Christianity, among other religious traditions, has been implicit over time for the disappearance of many "sheep."

---

[2] Luke 15:4-6 NRSV.

[3] Amy Jill Levine, *Short Stories by Jesus: The Enigmatic Parables of A Controversial Rabbi* (New York: Harper One, 2014), 33.

Perhaps this was the point of the parable of the lost sheep. What if the greatest lesson to be learned is not the sinfulness of the sheep, but rather the shamefulness of a community that sees itself as complete while one of its own is missing?

In her book, *Short Stories*, author Amy Jill Levine offers the following insightful take on the parable of the lost sheep:

> The sinner is the one who "breaks the Law," but the "Law" becomes understood not in terms of "Love your neighbor as yourself" or "Leave the corners of your field for the poor," but in terms of earning one's way to heaven, legalism, or works-righteousness. Many Christian readers, already primed to think of Law as the antithesis of grace and as a "burden," come to identify with the "sinner" who is freed from this dreadful legalism. Again, this is not what first-century (or twenty-first-century) Jews would hear. Similarly, there are no "outcasts" in any of the three parables in Luke 15. The shepherd did not expel the sheep for bleating a blasphemy or grazing on nonkosher grass. The sheep did not sin. Rather, the shepherd lost the sheep.[4]

Jesus telling a story about a person who owns one hundred sheep was most likely not something the average person could identify with. Anyone who could imagine being able to afford a hundred sheep would never dream of chasing down one that went missing while leaving the others unattended. Honestly, that's how the human heart works. If we had unlimited resources, say one hundred sheep, it would be almost impossible to even miss one let alone waste time worrying about the one that is missing if we lost it. So maybe one of the lessons we can learn from this story about a missing sheep is less about the shortcoming of a sheep and more

---

[4]Amy Jill Levine, *Short Stories by Jesus: The Enigmatic Parables of A Controversial Rabbi* (New York: Harper One, 2014), 33.

11

about the shortcomings of a community. Could it be that the idea of belonging to something greater can eventually lead to ignoring the individual completely?

What's amazing about this story is that the sheep doesn't suddenly realize the error of its ways. The sheep doesn't even ask for forgiveness. It is the shepherd who suddenly realizes that the community he guards is incomplete. "He notices the single missing sheep among the ninety-nine in the wilderness. For him, the missing sheep, whether it is one of a hundred or a million, makes the flock incomplete."[5]

The phenomenon of missing "sheep" is still an unspoken reality in the world today. Even more so, it is an unspoken reality in the community called Christianity. What makes this phenomenon so subtle is the prevailing attitude that still governs how we even interpret the story that Jesus tells. Those who are missing from the community are "sinners." It is the responsibility of those who are missing to change so that they are worthy of belonging.

Just like the sheep in the story, there are hundreds of people who find themselves outside of what appears to be the mainstream community, and the reality is, many of them feel the tremendous pressure to make changes that comply with the crowd in order to belong. I know this scenario all too well because my introduction to middle school quickly highlighted how different I was from my peers and how much stranger I was than others my age. The world I knew seemed to expand overnight, and the idea of going from being just one of a few sheep to one of hundreds was completely overwhelming. The result was that I intentionally disappeared.

It is becoming increasingly common for adults to be diagnosed with Asperger's syndrome, which for all intents and purposes is now considered a part of that autism spectrum disorder. I have spoken to several adults who have been recently diagnosed with

---

[5]Amy Jill Levine, *Short Stories by Jesus: The Enigmatic Parables of A Controversial Rabbi* (New York: Harper One, 2014), 41.

autism, and there are many just like me, who spent years trying their best to blend in and be like everyone else. In one sense, it is almost as though an entire generation of autistic children went completely unnoticed because, well, we disappeared into a sea of similarity, one that drowned out our differences because of indifference. We went missing, for many reasons but mostly because no one taught us that it was okay to be different.

I am clear now that I disappeared because I was different, and being different meant I was deficient. I disappeared because the person I was didn't seem to be enough. I disappeared because I discovered that no matter how hard I tried, I couldn't be like all the other sheep. I am not even certain I knew what was wrong with me, but everyone else seemed to know because the community appeared to be quite comfortable without me being a part of it. No one was sad about my disappearance. There was no shepherd to notice my absence. The other sheep seemed to be perfectly fine that I was missing. The community seemed to be complete without me, and that made me feel as though the real me, was unimportant and unwanted. No missing child alert was issued, and no one was looking for the real me, and eventually not only was no one looking for me, I stopped looking for me, too.

# CHAPTER 2
# LOST

As long as I can remember, I preferred to be alone. I never had a desire to surround myself with a crowd of people. Being alone was perfectly okay for me because solitude gave me the ability to enter into my own world. In my world, people didn't matter much, so what people thought of me wasn't important. My world was peaceful. My world was simple, and at the same time, my world was profound. If left alone for the right amount of time, there was almost no problem I couldn't solve in my world. Retreating to my world provided me with the opportunity to find the answers I needed to survive in the outside world.

Around the age of twelve or thirteen, I discovered that my need for solitude could be a huge asset to me. If I focused enough of my time and energy on my problem with the outside world, I could develop a plan to solve my problem. I often wonder what the missing sheep thought about when it went missing. Did the sheep blame itself? Did it want to return to the flock? Did it even know it was missing in the first place? Did the sheep just prefer to be alone? As a lost sheep, a sheep that went missing from the community at large, I wrestled with all of these questions. As I stated earlier, our cultural and religious background teaches us that it is the sheep's responsibility to fit in, and that's what I was taught. If I wanted to be a part of the outside world, I had to find a way to fit in. Even if fitting in wasn't exactly on the top of my list, it was better than being an outcast.

I was always a fairly intelligent child, even at an early age. Most of what I know and am able to accomplish socially is because I was an avid reader. Despite that, when it came to social skills, I lacked the natural abilities that others had. Growing up in and through middle school was a challenge for me socially, as with most middle school students. Being a bookworm and a skinny, nerdy, dark-skinned black boy increased the pressure tremendously.

It was around this age that I went into hiding. I think I had a few friends and a small support network within the halls of my school, but the reality is that, in retrospect, those friendships were far from authentic because the few people I did manage to relate to socially were not really getting the real me. Instead, they got a version of me that surfaced to protect me from being excommunicated from the flock. After all, the reason I was on the outside was my fault, so I took the responsibility of fixing it, which meant fixing me.

The "me" of my early teen years wasn't far from the real me. I still enjoyed the same hobbies, mainly books and video games. I discovered that video games could connect me with almost anyone my age, so my attention turned to learning how to become more of that personality than the book smart nerd who seemed to jeopardize my chances of fitting in. I think it was then that my plan for fitting in was born. I would learn to leave the real me behind when I was alone, and I would learn to become someone else when I surfaced.

The tragedy of poor self-image and self-worth is one that all young people face at some point in time in their developmental years. I, too, found myself a victim at a young age, a victim of feeling like an outsider, and like most lost sheep, I became afraid.

## I Am Afraid

Fear is a motivator for change. Fear demands change. Fear fuels change. The problem with fear is that the change it produces is always false. Fear cannot produce authentic change; only love can produce positive change. Fear cannot produce positive change because fear is the opposite of love. "This is why I remind you to fan into flames the spiritual gift God gave you when I laid my hands on you. For God has not given us a spirit of fear and timidity, but of power, love, and self-discipline."[6] Fear is the antithesis of God's design for humanity. When Paul writes to his young protégé Timothy, he suggests that the gifts of God, the gifts given by God that make him unique, are in direct competition with fear. The

---

[6]2 Timothy 1:6-7 NLT.

16

result of fear could very well be the subtle disappearance of all that makes a person uniquely created by God. In other words, when fear takes over, the person God created seems to slowly disappear.

One of my favorite Bible stories as a child is found in the book of Daniel. I can recall being taught the story of three courageous young men who choose to be thrown into a fiery furnace rather than compromise their relationship with their god. An inspiring story no doubt, but one the biggest inspirations found in the story is the story of the cruel king who ordered them thrown into the fire.

Just before the climactic scene in chapter three, we find the series of events that led to King Nebuchadnezzar's decision to throw these three men into the fire. In chapter two of the book of Daniel, King Nebuchadnezzar has a dream that shakes him to his core. The dream was so strange that the king wanted someone to not only interpret it, but also to first tell him what his dream was. "But the king said to the astrologers, 'I am serious about this. If you don't tell me what my dream was and what it means, you will be torn limb from limb, and your houses will be turned into heaps of rubble!'"[7]

Faced with an impossible task, the king's team of astrologers admitted that they did not have the ability to comply with the king's request. As you can imagine, this made the king furious, and he ordered that all the wise men of Babylon be executed. Unfortunately, this also meant Daniel and his friends. When the palace guard arrived at the home of Daniel, Daniel inquired as to what had brought about such a harsh decree from the king. After hearing about the king's dilemma, Daniel hurried to see the king and asked for more time to tell him what the dream meant. "Then Daniel went home and told his friends Hananiah, Mishael, and Azariah what had happened. He urged them to ask the God of heaven to show them his mercy by telling them the secret, so they would not be executed along with the other wise men of Babylon."[8]

---

[7]Daniel 2:5 NLT.

[8]Daniel 2:17-18 NLT.

That night, God revealed the king's dream to Daniel. The following morning, Daniel rushed off to see the king to inform him that he had the answers he was looking for. Standing before the king, Daniel admitted that no human being could possibly know what the king dreamed or what his dream meant, but Daniel gave credit to his god for giving him the interpretation of King Nebuchadnezzar's dream. Daniel's explanation as to why God would want the king to know the dream—"...because God wants you to understand what was in your heart."[9] The next part of the story is so important. In fact, understanding what happens next will help us to understand what is in our own hearts and why we so very often become completely lost.

Here is what Daniel said to King Nebuchadnezzar:

> Your Majesty, you are the greatest of kings. The God of heaven has given you sovereignty, power, strength, and honor. He has made you the ruler over all the inhabited world and has put even the wild animals and birds under your control. You are the head of gold. But after your kingdom comes to an end, another kingdom, inferior to yours, will rise to take your place."[10]

So what does all this mean anyway? Here is the most important part to remember about the king's dream. According to Daniel, God willingly and willfully gave King Nebuchadnezzar power. In fact, not only did he give the king power, but he made the king strong and honorable. The gold head of the statue represented Nebuchadnezzar. Now, we know King Nebuchadnezzar as a pretty horrible guy. After all, he was having his dream interpreted by Daniel, a slave he stole from a nation his army defeated. So Nebuchadnezzar was not a perfect man, yet God seemed to think pretty highly of him. So much so that God gave him power and

---

[9]Daniel 2:30 NLT.

[10]Daniel 2:37-39 NLT.

strength and then said that there will never be an earthly kingdom that will compare to King Nebuchadnezzar's kingdom.

King Nebuchadnezzar, according to God, would be a pretty important and pretty influential leader in the world. History would record him as being one of the best leaders the world has ever seen, and all this was possible even though King Nebuchadnezzar was far from perfect. I mean the king wasn't even a real "good" guy by our modern-day standards. The irony of it all is that despite his mistakes and his limitations, God established him as a great and historic leader, one whose kingdom could only be eclipsed by God's Kingdom. If you ask me, that makes Nebuchadnezzar a pretty special guy.

If God could assure you that despite your mistakes, your shortcomings, and your limitations, you would be great one day, how would you respond? Most people would probably respond the way King Nebuchadnezzar responded. "The king said to Daniel, 'Truly, your God is the greatest of gods, the Lord over kings, a revealer of mysteries, for you have been able to reveal this secret.'"[11] The king's response is pretty typical. When God gives us an identity, it tends to attract our allegiance. Humanity's greatest need from God is not miracles; our greatest need is God giving our lives meaning beyond merely avoiding mistakes and missteps.

What happens next is subtle and yet standard for most people. The next chapter of the story finds the king erecting an image of gold that he wants the entire country to worship:

> King Nebuchadnezzar made a gold statue ninety feet tall and nine feet wide and set it up on the plain of Dura in the province of Babylon. Then he sent messages to the high officers, officials, governors, advisers, treasurers, judges, magistrates, and all the provincial officials to come to the dedication of the statue he had set up. So all these officials came and stood before the statue King Nebuchadnezzar had

[11]Daniel 2:48 NLT.

set up. Then a herald shouted out, "People of all races and nations and languages, listen to the king's command! When you hear the sound of the horn, flute, zither, lyre, harp, pipes, and other musical instruments, bow to the ground to worship King Nebuchadnezzar's gold statue. Anyone who refuses will be immediately be thrown into a blazing furnace."[12]

According to many scholars and Bible experts, King Nebuchadnezzar's statue was likely an image of himself. In Daniel's interpretation of the king's dream, only the statue's head was gold. The golden head represented King Nebuchadnezzar, yet somehow in the next chapter of his life, he found himself dissatisfied with the person God had created him to be. The ninety-foot golden image he erected was the result of his greatest fear—the fear of not being enough.

We all share the same fear that Nebuchadnezzar wrestled with. Sometime between his original dream in chapter two and his creation of a ninety-foot image in chapter three, he was no longer convinced that he was enough. The result of his fear is the result of our fear. When we fear we are not enough, we create false images of ourselves, images that often overcompensate for our deepest fear that no matter how good God thinks we are, it is not enough for us.

## Fear and False Images

When I was in middle school, the fear of not being enough finally took its grip on my life. The fear of not being enough wrapped its fingers around my throat and squeezed with enough force to finally squeeze the life out of me. My life, the life that God had given me, the life that was complete with imperfections and weaknesses, began to disappear. What began to emerge was an image. I was not a ninety-foot statue, but it was a larger-than-life false representation of the real me nonetheless.

---

[12]Daniel 3:1-6 NLT.

One of the first signs that I was erecting a false image was the decline of my academic interest. I had always been a great student growing up. I loved to read. I enjoyed learning. I can remember the feeling of accomplishment and joy when I was able to grasp new ideas and new concepts. One of my favorite subjects was history. I particularly enjoyed biographies and documentaries. I found something intriguing about the stories of historic people and places. Even more than fiction, the life stories of historical figures captured my imagination in ways that nothing else could. Education was my gateway into the world. Education was my strength; it was where I found value. School was the place where I could prove I was more than just an odd bird who didn't socialize much; school made me special.

All that seemed to change in middle school. As it turned out, being smart and being a bookworm didn't make me special, it made me stupid. I never did quite understand the irony of how being smart in middle school could make me feel so stupid and ignorant. It felt as though the more visible my academic achievements were, the more violent middle school became. Middle school was violent because any attempt to change a person without love is an act of violence. The moment I stopped loving myself was the moment I became violent and dangerous, not to others, but to myself.

I once heard a story of a man isolated on a deserted island for years. Realizing he would be on the island for an extended period of time, he decided to make himself some shelter. The story goes on to say that after some time had lapsed, another man washed up on the shore of this remote deserted island. After spending years alone on the island, the first man was excited to see another human being. Running up to his new visitor, he said, "I am so excited to see another human being after all these years. Let me show you around the island!" The man quickly grabbed his new friend by the hand and dragged him to a location on the island where there were three huts made from sticks, trees, and mud. The second man was puzzled by the three dwellings and asked the first man, "What are the three huts for?" The first man quickly responded, "I knew I would be here a while, so I decided I needed to make myself some shelter. The first hut is my home." "Great" the second man replied, "What is the hut in the middle?" The first man replied, "Well, I am a devout Christian, so I knew I would need a place to worship. The second hut is my church." "Great," the second man replied. "I am a Christian, too. May I ask what the third hut is for?" "Oh," said the first man, "that's the church I used to attend."

Life for many people is similar to the story of this man. We can blame the world for our lack of peace when the reality is that we have a more difficult time getting along with ourselves than we do getting along with others. Bullying played a role in my life over those years, but if I were to be honest, the person who was most violent toward me was myself. I wasn't able to have a healthy relationship with myself. No one person made me feel as bad and as worthless as I made myself feel. When we are unhappy with who we are and how God made us, it leads to a massive downward spiral into violence against self. While I never turned to self-harm as a means of violence against myself, I did change who I was because I was unhappy with how I was made. I was unhappy with the fact that no matter how hard I tried, I could not be as outgoing as the other kids my age. I was terribly unhappy with how socially inept I seemed to be. I was painfully unhappy about the fact that being smart was not cool and definitely not popular. The thought of being different made me feel deficient.

Now, what I am about to say next will most likely go against most of your traditional view of faith and maybe even your traditional view of sin, but before you completely abandon ship, I want you to take a close look at the perspective I am offering, and determine for yourself if it even remotely explains our human proclivity to behave badly. Are you ready? Being "lost" is not about bad behavior; being lost is the result of doing a bad job of being someone that God didn't create you to be. You will always fail at being someone you were not meant to be. The result of the continued failure to be someone you are not is the bad behavior (sin) that is merely an effort to make ourselves less deficient, less depressed, or less different than everyone else. Sin is the result of a continued dissatisfaction with who God made us to be.

If you're a Christian, then you can trace this idea back to the beginning of our understanding of sin. In the beginning, God created a place that literally meant paradise; it was the perfect scenario. Even if you can't picture a garden as being the perfect place for you, feel free to substitute it with a location and an environment that speaks to you. The point is that, as Adam and Eve knew it, things were perfect. God had set them both up with a stellar situation. In fact, it was so great that there was no pressure to perform or compare. Adam and Eve were just fine where they were.

One of the most interesting observations in this story is that as perfect as things were, the idea of boundaries still existed. Now what this suggests to me, and it should to you, is that life with boundaries is a part of what makes life enjoyable. God had only one rule, "But the Lord God warned him, 'You may freely eat the fruit of every tree in the garden—except the tree of the knowledge of good and evil. If you eat its fruit, you are sure to die.'"[13] The issue here is that although life comes with boundaries, God still provides all the ingredients needed to enjoy life. In essence, faith in God was never designed to focus on how not to break the rules; faith in God is the source by which we can most effectively enjoy the life that he has prepared for us to enjoy. We don't cross the boundaries or sin because God has not provided a means to satisfy his creation; we cross boundaries and sin because we become dissatisfied with who we are. Let's take a closer look at the creation narrative:

> The serpent was the shrewdest of all the wild animals the Lord God had made. One day he asked the woman, "Did God really say you must not eat the fruit from any of the trees in the garden?" "Of course we may eat fruit from the trees in the garden," the woman replied. "It's only the fruit from the tree in the middle of the garden that we are not allowed

---

[13]Genesis 2:16 NLT.

to eat." God said, "You must not eat it or even touch it; if you do, you will die."[14]

Let's pause for just a moment. At this point, things are going fairly well. Granted, Eve takes a few liberties with God's instructions when she added that they shouldn't touch the fruit at all, but honestly who hasn't struggled to memorize a verse in the Bible? In my opinion, she doesn't necessarily disagree with God, or even feel the need to disobey God. Life is good, they have all the fruit that they can eat, and focusing on the one tree that God doesn't want them to eat from (or touch) doesn't seem like the best way to enjoy the paradise God has prepared for them. What happens next is what happens to us all.

> "You won't die!" the serpent replied to the woman. "God knows that your eyes will be opened as soon as you eat it, and you will be like God, knowing both good and evil." The woman was convinced. She saw that the tree was beautiful and its fruit looked delicious, and she wanted the wisdom it could give her. So she took some of the fruit and ate it. Then she gave some to her husband who was with her, and he ate it, too. At that moment their eyes were opened, and they suddenly felt shame at their nakedness. [15]

Although life as they knew it was perfect, the idea that there was something they lacked that God had either neglected or refused to give them drove them to cross a critical boundary. The serpent was successful in getting them to become dissatisfied with how God had created them. He tempted them with the idea that eating the fruit would somehow make them more perfect, as if God had designed them as incomplete and inferior beings. God is perfect. He is incapable of doing anything less than perfectly. This means that even with all of your flaws, shortcomings, and issues, you are still God's perfect creation.

---

[14]Genesis 3:1-3.

[15]Genesis 3:4-7 NLT.

I was nearly thirty-seven years old before I could fully embrace who God made me to be. I spent years struggling with who I was and how I was made and why I even existed, because for the most part, I was was not satisfied with the idea that I was never designed to be just like everyone else. The harsh reality is that there are millions of people who feel the exact same way. I am not alone in the wondering, wandering, and worrying about how to live a life of purpose. What I have discovered, however, is that living with purpose first requires an understanding of who I am as a person.

One of the reasons it was extremely difficult for me to understand who I was as a person was that I was extremely young at that time I went missing. I was so afraid of not being enough that I allowed myself to become another person, mostly because being a teenager in middle school means barely knowing how to find your next class, let alone finding out who you are.

Right up until the time I went missing, I was okay with who I was. I was a smart kid who loved to read and who made excellent grades. In elementary school, I was placed in the talented and gifted program, and I always made A's. In my earlier years of middle school, I was invited to join the National Junior Honor Society. While I can appreciate this distinguished honor now, I can recall how this pivotal moment in my life history marked the beginning stages of my disappearing act.

For some unknown reason, I was extremely embarrassed about being chosen for this honor. I literally had to be dragged to the ceremony for the induction because I did not want to attend, let alone actually be a part of the National Junior Honor Society. The power of fear, particularly the fear of not being enough, will always result in failing to embrace validation for being your true self. Here I was, being honored for being the smart, intelligent bookworm I was created to be, but I did not and could not appreciate it because I was afraid I was not the person that everyone else said I should be. Fear of not being enough destroys our ability to eventually become the best version of who God created us to be.

Author and pastor, John Ortberg, outlines the seven most common versions of self in his book *The Me I Want to Be: Becoming God's Best Version of You.*

1.  The Me I Don't Want to Be
2.  The Me I Pretend to Be
3.  The Me I Think I Should Be
4.  The Me Other People Want Me to Be
5.  The Me I'm Afraid God Wants
6.  The Me That Fails to Be
7.  The Me I am Meant to Be[16]

If you're anything like me, you probably feel as though you could fit into any one of the above categories. It is highly possible that, given the situation and the relationship, I can be more than one "me." Perhaps that is why it is often so exhausting when we constantly live life trying to be someone that God has not created us to be.

What we learn from Adam and Eve is that crossing boundaries in an effort to make ourselves something other than what we were created to be always leaves us feeling ashamed. Most of my regrets in life are connected to how I tried so desperately to be someone I wasn't, and the lengths to which I went to create that person. Creating a new person is hard work. Actually, creating a new person is painful and life taking. Just ask Jesus. New life requires death, and Jesus died so that we could receive new life in him. The problem is that when we attempt to create a new person without Jesus, we end up going to great and dangerous lengths to become something and someone different. The lengths to which we are willing to go will eventually cost us our life unless we find the courage to live as we were created.

---

[16]John Ortberg, *The Me I Want to Be* (Grand Rapids: Zondervan, 2010), 22-30.

# CHAPTER 3
# I AM MISERABLE

## Downward Spiral

Living as someone else requires a tremendous amount of energy. The energy needed to become someone else and maintain that image is unnatural, and at some point, that energy will be unavailable. I soon discovered this harsh reality as I stumbled out of middle school and into my high school years.

Middle school was tough, but I somehow managed to create an image that was just effective enough to keep me going. The problem was that after about three years of this charade, I began to run out of energy. My emotional, spiritual, and mental energy had become depleted. I knew that there was no possible way I could continue at the pace I had set for myself. I had set unrealistic expectations of myself, and now the seeds of those expectations were beginning to grow and spread like weeds, choking out my moral and ethical judgment. One of the greatest tragedies of the fear of not being enough is the erosion of ethical and moral standards.

By the time I had entered high school, I had committed myself to competing in the comparison game. Middle school was a training ground for what would be the real challenge, a challenge that all teens face and few adults ever escape. The challenge of constantly comparing ourselves to others leads us down the road of conformity. On the surface, this may seem to be merely a routine part of growing up and learning to cope with a cruel world that categorizes people by comparing them to others; however, the implications are often crippling. Nothing is more debilitating in life than a constant depreciation of self-value. Whether you realize it or not, you were created with a divine intrinsic value that makes you special no matter how different you feel or how deficient others make you feel.

My wife and I have three beautiful and very active boys. One of the most interesting things about being a parent to young children is that I am constantly learning new things about God, about myself, and about life by listening to the very profound, and sometimes hilarious, statements that our sons make. On one occasion, our middle son, who was five at the time, was losing baby teeth. Although losing teeth is very common for a kid his age, the way he approached the situation was anything but common. In fact, his uncommon approach to valuating his lost tooth is what helped me gain a clear understanding of how little we often value ourselves.

After pulling his own tooth (something I would have never done at his age), my son wanted to sit down and write a letter to the tooth fairy. At the time, I supposed the intention was simply to provide a brief introduction and to thank the tooth fairy for her gift. He grabbed my wife, and they spent the next twenty minutes crafting the perfect letter for the tooth fairy. After they had completed the letter, my wife insisted that I read it. While I was honestly not interested in reading the letter, I would soon discover something in it that would eventually change my life. The note that my son had written to the tooth fairy read, "Dear Tooth Fairy. I would like forty dollars."

Two things are important about this hilarious exchange. First, my son wanted the forty dollars so that he could give his brother twenty. An extremely nice gesture on his part, but even if he was attempting to help out his older brother, it would still mean he was appraising his tooth, a baby tooth no less, at twenty dollars. That's a pretty steep price for a tooth. (For the record, he received two dollars from the tooth fairy.) Second, I learned the importance of properly valuing the things that God placed inside me.

My son seemed to understand this principle at a much younger age than I did. In reality, he probably understood it more than most teenagers and young adults. The idea that he could place such a high dollar amount on such a small tooth suggests that he understood that some things are valuable simply because God created them that way.

That's a lesson I didn't have the good fortune of learning at his age. Had I learned that lesson, I would not have spent most of my teenage years as a miserable person trying to cope with not measuring up to the world's expectations of me. I hadn't learned that lesson. I hadn't known that it even existed, and, unlike the saying, what I didn't know *did* hurt me.

Three years of pretending left me tired. I had run out of personas to imitate, and I had run out of the natural energy to do it. The beginning of my high school years found me in a dark and lonely place. I was alone, but not because I wanted to be. This time, I felt alone because of what I so desperately wanted to *be*. Wanting to be something and someone different as a high school freshman meant that I would have to take my false image to the next level, and that next level meant finding something to fuel my fake personality. That something became drugs and alcohol.

I was a freshman in high school the first time I encountered drugs. In those days, I didn't actually know anyone who used drugs. Growing up in the military meant everything I knew was based on military culture. In many ways, my siblings and I were exposed to a lot—we had the opportunity to see different countries, experience a variety of cultures, and try new and exciting things. On the other hand, we were also extremely sheltered. I won't say I was completely unaware of the existence of illegal drugs, but the harsh reality was that as a military brat, I just wasn't exposed to certain things, and drugs was one of them. It's no wonder that the first time I even heard the term marijuana was a few years after my father had retired and we had settled into civilian life in Texas.

Life at age fourteen was difficult. It was the perfect storm—the exposure of a sensitive and shy kid with no self-confidence to a new world of drugs and alcohol. Like most people, I did not just wake up and decide I wanted to start smoking pot. As I stated earlier, I didn't even know what the stuff was and probably wouldn't have recognized it if someone had put it in my hand. Most of my life had been lived under an umbrella of naivety, but the storm known as high school was simply too much for that fragile umbrella to cover.

When I got to high school, I began making more friends. I think a large part of this was simply because the population was much larger. Eventually, I would have a car in high school, so I could make more friends by playing the statistical odds. With so many students in one location, I was bound to meet some people I could connect with. For the most part, I was fairly social, but looking back, I can see it made me all the wrong types of friends, mainly because I was just as naïve about people as I was about the drugs that they would eventually offer me.

I've struggled with this part of my life and story for one primary reason: I have never wanted to think of myself as someone who was addicted to drugs. Understand that part of that is the culture we live in, and the other part is the result of being a kid who was so empty that using substances to alter my personality type actually felt like a gift, a gift given to me to help me become the person that God had somehow neglected to make me. In many ways, drug use was a direct result of my lack of faith in God. By the time I got to high school, I was tired of pretending to be someone I wasn't, and I was blaming God for my exhaustion. It was time to take matters into my own hands. God had failed me, and I was wounded.

## Doubting Thomas

When life hands you lemons, make lemonade. That's what we're taught, and that's what we believe. No matter where you find yourself on your spiritual journey, you will encounter periods of life when you're handed circumstances that are far beyond your control. When that happens, any faith you have will take a hit. One of the most interesting and well-known figures in Christianity is Thomas. Christians and non-Christians alike know the name of Thomas because he is most known for his doubts.

Despite his reputation for being a skeptic, Thomas actually wasn't a bad guy. For some reason, we always tend to find it difficult to see people past their momentary lapses in judgment or faith. Thomas is an example of that. Although Thomas was the disciple that would go on to take the gospel into India, we seem to connect him to one small chapter in his life when he struggled to believe.

Thomas was an extremely loyal person. I can relate to that. I don't have many close friends, but the close friends I do have, I have had for a very long time. Thomas was also extremely loyal to Jesus. It is the often untold part of his life, but Thomas wasn't a superficial, skeptical Christ follower the way we have characterized him. In fact, Thomas was the guy who was willing to give his life to and for his friend Jesus.

In John chapter eleven, Jesus gets word that his very close friend Lazarus is sick. Lazarus lived in Bethany with his sisters Mary and Martha. Although John records that Jesus intentionally stayed where he was for two days after receiving the news about Lazarus, he would eventually make plans to go back to Judea. The only problem was that their last encounter in Judea was not a favorable one.

> Finally, he said to his disciples, "Let's go back to Judea." But his disciples objected. "Rabbi," they said, "only a few days ago the people in Judea where trying to stone you. Are you going there again?" Jesus replied, "There are twelve hours of daylight every day. During the day people can walk safely. They can see because they have the light of this world. But at night there is danger of stumbling because they have no light." Then he said, "Our friend Lazarus has fallen asleep, but now I will go and wake him up." The disciples said, "Lord, if he is sleeping, he will soon get better!" They thought Jesus meant Lazarus was simply sleeping, but Jesus meant Lazarus had died. So he told them plainly, "Lazarus is dead. And for your sakes, I'm glad I wasn't there, for now you will really believe. Come, let's go see

him." Thomas, nicknamed the Twin, said to his fellow disciples, *"Let's go, too—and die with Jesus."*[17]

While we don't know much about Thomas, this recorded incident speaks volumes about the type of person he was. Out of all the disciples present during this discussion about returning to Judea, Thomas was the only one who appeared to have the courage to make the trip back with Jesus. Now, some scholars believe that perhaps Thomas was a pessimist, and his reaction was simply a negative attitude mixed with a bit of sarcasm about the whole idea of facing certain death in Judea, but I disagree. Thomas appears to be courageous, not cowardly. We can hardly characterize someone willing to die with and for Jesus as a coward and a doubter.

So what happened to Thomas that caused him to doubt the resurrection of Jesus? What happened to the man who was so courageous that he was willing to travel the distance with Jesus to Judea to possibly face death? What I am about share next is conjecture at best, yet I believe it is something we must take into consideration before we characterize Thomas based on a snapshot in biblical history that may not represent him for who he really was.

I think Thomas struggled with the idea of a resurrected Jesus for two primary reasons. It is extremely hard to hope when you are hurting, and it is difficult to believe in anything when you are broken. Let's be honest, no one really believed that Jesus was going to rise from his grave three days after his brutal execution. Thomas was not any more or any less a doubter than any of his colleagues. Most of the close group of men and women who followed Jesus for three-plus years as his disciples had abandoned all hope. Their mentor and teacher was gone, the movement was over, and they were all grieving a tremendous loss.

Thomas, like many of the others, was extremely hurt. Remember, Thomas was the one who was willing to die with Jesus, a sign that perhaps at least at that time he was one of the most

---

[17]John 11:7-16 NLT.

committed of Jesus' followers. What can be seen about Thomas and his commitment to Jesus can only expose us to the depths of pain he probably felt at having lost someone to whom he was extremely loyal. After all, Thomas had been willing to give his life for Jesus, and now Jesus was gone.

Thomas was fully aware of the brutality they put his friend through when he was beaten and executed. That means that Thomas was angry, afraid, and perhaps more than anything else, he felt alone. Simply put, Thomas was a severely wounded man, and it is hard to hope when you've been hurt, and it is extremely difficult to believe in anything when you have been emotionally and spiritually broken. It is, then, no wonder that Thomas was obsessed with wounds. When his colleagues approached him about encountering the resurrected Christ, all Thomas could focus on was a need to see the wounds.

In the summer of 2012, I tore my right Achilles tendon while playing basketball with the youth group from my church. If you have ever torn a tendon, then you know it is extremely painful and extremely debilitating. After the immediate shock of realizing what I had done, I was able to pull myself together enough to make it home and have my wife take me to the emergency room. It was there that they confirmed the tear, and the next step was finding a doctor to surgically repair my right leg. Eventually, I went on to have the surgery, and after months of being immobile, I started physical therapy to begin the process of strengthening my leg so that I could function normally again.

What's intriguing about the entire process is that I began to have an obsession with my woundedness. Not only did I tend to focus a lot of time and energy on how hurt I was, I also became obsessed with other people's injuries. I began to notice more sports stories about athletes with various injuries, and I was extremely intrigued to learn about people who had suffered the same type of injury I had. To add to the equation, I began to notice that other parts of me began to hurt. I started to develop knee, hip, and back pain that I had never experienced before. When one part of you hurts, it always leads to other parts of you hurting.

Thomas was hurt. Thomas was wounded. His friend had been brutally murdered, and he was emotionally and spiritual hurt, and as a result, other parts of him began hurting. I once heard a pastor say "Hurt people *hurt* people." While I couldn't agree more, I want to add to that phrase by saying that hurt people *hunt* hurt people.

When I was at the peak of my hurt and disappointment resulting from my physical injury, I actively hunted for others who had been hurt in the same way that I had been hurt. Something about human nature causes us to find comfort in the idea that we are not the only ones who have experienced the pain we so often encounter in life. When you've been deeply wounded, all you want to know is that there is someone else who is hurting as badly as you are. I know what you're thinking. It's an awful thing to want someone else to hurt just because you are hurting, but it is the raw, honest truth about being emotionally and spiritually wounded. I guess the saying is true—misery really does love company.

So maybe Thomas wasn't such a bad guy after all. Like many of us, he may have just been experiencing pain so deep that his need to not be alone in his agony caused him to become obsessed with wounds. Hurting people hunt for other hurting people. The only way to satisfy his wounded soul was to see the wounds that Jesus experienced. After all, the other disciples had an opportunity to experience it the first time Jesus appeared, and Thomas missed out on the opportunity of a lifetime.

When one part of you hurts, it starts hurting other parts of you. One of the most significant injuries Thomas incurred was a missed opportunity. While his heart and soul were still riddled with grief stemming from missing his friend and mentor Jesus, he gets word that Jesus has returned from the dead, and he missed that as well. The thing that wounded me the most when I tore my Achilles tendon was all the opportunities I missed while sitting at home recovering from my surgery. I missed taking my children to school and picking them up every day. I missed the people at my church, the youth group I led, and the time I invested in their young lives. It seemed like all the activities I was in charge of suffered because of my absence, and while I may have been imagining the importance of my role in all the things I was missing, the fact still remains that whenever you feel you are missing out on an opportunity in life, it leaves you wounded.

Thomas didn't really expect any type of special treatment. He just wanted to experience Jesus for himself. He felt wounded by the fact that not only had he been missing his friend, but he had missed his chance with him again. Remember, it's hard to hope when you're hurting, and it's much harder to believe when you've been broken. Like Thomas, many of us struggle to believe because life has broken us and stripped us of all hope, and that is cause for doubt in even the most optimistic person. So maybe Thomas wasn't as much of a doubter as we have made him out to be. Maybe he was just wounded by missing Jesus and missing opportunities.

When I began using drugs and alcohol at a young age, I was miserable on the inside. My faith was shattered by the idea that I was missing something. While I can clearly see now that my lack of faith came from being a very wounded soul, all I knew at age fourteen was that something and someone was missing. My life seemed to be a series of missed opportunities, opportunities that everyone else experienced. Like Thomas, I felt wounded and alone, and since I was hurting, I went on the hunt to find people who were just as hurt as I was. The result was that I began to engage in behavior that felt like the answer, only to reveal itself as one more contributor to my problem.

## Defining Moments

Thankfully, my story did not end in pain. I am fortunate. Many other kids suffer in silence and then seek to medicate themselves into an emotional and spiritual stupor that will eliminate the pain associated with being deeply wounded. Drugs and alcohol were my vices, but some children turn to other expressions of self-harm such as cutting and self-mutilation, illicit and experimental sexual practices, and other extreme risky behavior. Like Thomas, I was at a place in life where I was struggling tremendously with my faith, yet my wounds would not win the battle for my heart and mind. Eventually, I would have my own experience with faith that would change my life for the better.

I would continue my destructive behavior until I reached my freshman year in college. How I made it to college is a miracle story in and of itself, and a testament to God's gentle and loving hand guiding me throughout every stage of my young and wounded life, even when I did not discern it or deserve it. That's how God works, and that's exactly how Jesus dealt with a wounded and doubting disciple Thomas. Instead of condemning him for his momentary flash of humanity, Jesus exposed Thomas to his own wounds, and by doing so, exposed Thomas to his own humanity.

> One of the twelve disciples, Thomas (nicknamed the Twin), was not with the others when Jesus came. They told him, "We have seen the Lord!" But he replied, "I won't believe it unless I see the nail wounds in his hands, put my fingers into them and place my hand into the wound in his side." Eight days later the disciples were together again, this time Thomas was with them. The doors were locked; but suddenly, as before, Jesus was standing among them. "Peace be with you," he said. Then he said to Thomas, "Put your finger here, and look at my hands. Put your hand into the wound in my side. Don't be faithless any longer. Believe!" "My Lord and my God!" Thomas exclaimed. Then Jesus told him, "You believe because you have seen me. Blessed are those who believe without seeing me."[18]

---

[18] John 20:24:29 NLT.

This encounter, the encounter with a resurrected Jesus, was without question a defining moment in the life of Thomas. Jesus just seemed to show up one day in a room full of his followers and, after greeting them, he turned to Thomas and asked him to do the exact thing that Thomas had early declared would destroy his doubt. It seems as though Jesus, even though not present when Thomas made the statements, knew exactly what Thomas needed in order to gain a sense of security and serenity in his life.

The message of the gospel is a defining moment. It is the moment when humanity and divinity collide, and humanity gets that greatest glimpse into the ability of God to identify with his creation. Thomas needed what most of us need; we simply need to know that God knows how much we hurt, how miserable we really are, and how much He hurts as a result of our misery. Knowing that Jesus also hurts, and that the reason why he hurts is because we hurt—that is a defining moment. The idea that Jesus has wounds, and that he is willing to expose his wounds to those of us who have struggled to believe in him, speaks volumes, especially when you struggle to relationally connect with people.

As I stated earlier, I grew up in the church. Whether I realized it at the time or not, the church had a tremendous influence on my life. That's a huge reason why I still believe in the local church. Despite all of her flaws and inconsistencies, the church is the plan that Jesus left for his followers. It was because of the local church that I was exposed at an early age to ideas and concepts about faith. It would take me a while to make the crucial connection between how hurt I was, how hurt Jesus was for me, and how I hurt others in the process.

In 1996, I graduated from high school, and I still struggled with using drugs and alcohol. I wish I could tell you I had found a reason to stop earlier, but I didn't. Like Thomas, I was hurting, and I needed a defining moment to change my life, a moment where faith became more than an idea and a concept, a moment where, like Thomas, I could understand Jesus as "My Lord and my God."[19]

In the fall of 1996, I began my college football career at Concordia University Wisconsin. Thanks to the concern of a former high school coach, I was offered the opportunity to attend college and play football. Looking back, I can see the blessing and benefit of being able to leave home and pursue my education. On the other hand, a broken and wounded soul now left to figure out life in a foreign land was almost a recipe for my own downfall.

College was a world of confusion for me. There was definitely an entirely new level of social expectations that I was unable to manage. Playing on the football team in college raised the stakes of social pressure. Even in a small school like Concordia University Wisconsin, I felt the pressure of being a person that I wasn't. Socializing with people was difficult—actually, extremely difficult—and the only answer I could come up with in order to cope was to increase my use of drugs and alcohol. I was in the greatest fight of my life, trying so desperately to become someone I wasn't, and my efforts eventually worked. I was totally lost, and the person I had become was the worst version of myself. "The Holy Spirit is always ready to guide you toward God's best version of yourself." [20] I needed guidance, but the way that God would eventually direct me toward becoming his version of me would be in the form of a very traumatic experience.

## Just like Jonah

One of the greatest defining moments in the Bible is found in the epic story of Jonah. Both Christians and non-Christians are familiar with this epic story—no one can resist a story in which a man is swallowed by a gigantic fish. Buried beneath the surface of an

---

[19] John 20:24:29 NLT.

[20] John Ortberg, *The Me I Want to Be* (Grand Rapids: Zondervan, 2010), 44.

entertaining story, however, is an education about running from the responsibility of being the person God may be calling you to become.

> The Lord gave the message to Jonah son of Amittai: "Get up and go to the city of Nineveh. Announce my judgment against it because I have seen how wicked its people are." But Jonah got up and went in the opposite direction to get away from the Lord. He went down to the port of Joppa, where he found a ship leaving for Tarshish. He bought a ticket and went on board, hoping to escape from the Lord by sailing to Tarshish.[21]

This story resonates with me. In many ways, it is a direct reflection of my life and relationship with God during the earliest years of my college experience. My story, however, is not unique. Many people spend an enormous amount of time and energy trying to escape the responsibility of being the person God is calling them to be. One of the most tragic mistakes we make in life is clearly hearing and understanding the direction we need to go, and yet intentionally heading in the opposite direction.

I'm not sure exactly what caused Jonah to go the other way. The opening sentences of his story don't give us any insight into his thought process, but I'm almost certain it was a direct reflection of his strained relationship with God because he "went in the opposite direction to get away from the *Lord*."[22] Perhaps you've been in his position before. I have, and getting away from God was the result of my lack of faith in God, not because of who He was or even who He was not. I was looking to get as far away from God as I could because I was dissatisfied with who I was, not who God was.

---

[21]Jonah 1:1-3 NLT.

[22]Ibid.

Like Jonah, I was "hoping to escape from the Lord,"[23] thinking that the further away I got from anything remotely religious, the better off I would be. After all, God was responsible for making me flawed and imperfect. God was responsible for me being so weak and fragile. It was God's doing that caused me to have the significant social struggles I had and, like Jonah, I had decided to try my hand at escaping my reality by escaping God.

In both Jonah's story and my story, we both considered running to be a viable option to deal with our identity issues. Most people do consider it the most viable option in similar circumstances. What runners usually fail to realize is that running from God almost always ends up involving innocent people. "But the Lord hurled a powerful wind over the sea, causing a violent storm that threatened to break the ship apart. Fearing for their lives, the desperate sailors shouted to their gods for help and threw the cargo overboard to lighten the ship."[24]

Jonah's decision to run away from God had consequences, but unlike most people, those who run from God usually have very little sense of self-worth, so the idea of facing consequences for their personal actions is not as strong as their need avoid them at all cost. Jonah didn't even embrace the idea of going to tell others about the consequences for rejecting God. How could he possibly be concerned about his own life? It wasn't until Jonah had a sense of how his actions affected his shipmates that he began to contemplate the idea that running away would not resolve his issues. Such was the case for me. I faced a defining moment, my very own "Jonah" experience during my retreat away from God's calling to be the person he created me to be.

During the fall of my sophomore year, I had my defining moment. It was the weekend of an away game, and due to an injury, I was not on the active roster to play that weekend. The head coach

---

[23]Jonah 1:3 NLT.

[24]Jonah 1:4-5 NLT.

of our football team had given me the choice to travel with the team regardless of my injury or to stay behind. Honestly, at this stage, I was far less serious about my athletic career, mostly because my focus was on maintaining the persona I had created just to fit in as a college athlete. Since I knew I wasn't going to play in the game, I secretly decided to use this opportunity to test out my new persona by staying behind and attending a few parties.

Now I won't go into all the gritty details of the activities of my weekend, but what I will share is the moment that God spoke to me and changed my life forever. After leaving a party with a few friends, I jumped in the car with our ride. I am certain that our driver did not drink any alcohol the entire night. I spent all of my time watching him, and I am confident that alcohol was not a factor in what I am about to tell you because we were never arrested for driving under the influence. This moment, this defining moment, was completely under God's influence, and it was a moment that changed my life.

While driving down the road, approaching a traffic light, I noticed from the backseat of the car that the light that we were approaching had changed from green to red. There was no yellow in between to warn the driver to begin slowing down in anticipation for a red light. I'm uncertain if the driver saw it because it was at that moment that the world, at least for me, slipped into what felt like a slow-motion movie. I could see and hear everything with such distinction and clarity that it was almost as if I had suddenly developed super powers.

At this point, our vehicle was far enough away from the light so that I could see the strange change take place, but we were not far enough away for the driver to have time to come to a complete stop. Our car went straight through the red light without hesitation and was suddenly sideswiped by a car on our right. The sheer force and impact of the car propelled us into a tailspin. I vividly remember the glass from the broken window launching into the air toward me. The cold air from the outside began to pour into the car, and then, suddenly, there was a second impact.

41

We had been hit by a second car. This time, the trajectory sent us into a more rapid spin, one that would eventually cause us to leap the median and move across this four-lane highway into oncoming traffic. Oncoming cars sped past us as I stared into their headlights. Not one car hit us directly, although it felt as though I could feel the vibrations of the other cars that were whizzing past us at high speeds. Then, without warning, all the sounds of screaming passengers and screeching tires and brakes suddenly stopped, and for what seemed like an eternity, all I heard was complete and utter silence.

I remember thinking that I had died or was about to die. Perhaps, in a sense, I did die that night, but it wasn't the accident that killed me, and it wasn't the person writing this that died. It was the image I had created, and it was God's voice that killed him. As clear and plain as anyone could possibly hear a voice, I heard what I know was the voice of the creator exclaim, "Everyone in this car is going to lose their life because of *your* disobedience."

Let me be clear, I'm not certain that God was actually going to kill everyone in the car, but at the same time, I was spiritually awakened to the devastating consequences of my continual denial of self, and the continued practice of perpetuating a false image that I created an addiction to maintain. What was real to me was that for the first time, I realized that my life mattered so much that my negative actions had a tremendous impact on the people to whom I was connected. That was for me a defining moment in the greatest sense of the concept. Despite how I felt about myself, I was destined to impact the lives of other people. How that impact would materialize depended upon my decision to answer the call of God to be myself.

# CHAPTER 4
# I AM DIFFERENT

## Choose Your Own Adventure

By now you've already heard me declare my love for books. That love and fascination with literature developed at a very early age. Growing up, I loved all types of books. I developed a love for information and insight through reading. It wasn't unusual for me to be seen reading the encyclopedia. I also loved history and biographies. Reading the amazing stories of people much more popular than myself helped give me insight into the social world and what it had to offer. Reading was a great tool that helped me to understand the world around me. When I wanted to recreate my own reality, I turned to *Choose Your Own Adventure* books, a type of book that was extremely popular when I was a child.

From birth, I was a different type of child. My sister reports that I had tremendous struggles with being left to the care of someone other than my mother. I would cry for hours on end because I was unable to adjust to other adults or children when my mother was not present. For the most part, that trend continued all the way through my early years. Then I learned to talk and read. I loved "choose your own adventure" books because, unlike my life, I could decide how the story would end.

The ability to control the story is probably is appealing to many people. Given the opportunity, I would return to a certain point in my story and choose something different for myself. I think most people would take that opportunity. It's only natural to wish that some parts of your story had turned out differently.

Most of the decisions we make are because we are given the freedom to make those decisions. It's natural to want to change things if we have the power to do so. Unfortunately, a large portion of the things we try to change about our story simply cannot be changed. Instead, we choose to alter as much as we can in hopes that the story will end differently this time.

When I opened a *Choose Your Own Adventure* book, I had the power and control necessary to guide the story. My decisions developed the plot with all of its twists and turns. Human beings love control. The more fixed our story is from birth, the more we crave the ability to control the outcome. We all wish we could choose our own adventure.

When you understand that you're different, especially as a child, you understand that many stories end in a similar fashion. People who are different get picked on. People who are different don't get voted most popular. People who are different definitely don't get the girl or guy of their dreams, and people who are different don't get the ending they are often desperately chasing. So it should not take you by surprise when I say that deep down inside, no one really wants to be different because the lives of those of us who are dramatically different usually don't end up where we dreamed they would.

John the Baptist is almost a cultural and religious icon, especially during his lifetime. Today his name rings on well past his entrance to the grave. Many people considered him a hero of the faith and the man who introduced the world to Jesus by baptizing him. Who else can say they had the honor and privilege of baptizing Jesus? That title and distinction belongs to one man and one man only, John the Baptist.

We don't know an awful lot about John. We have bits and pieces of his incredible life story, but one of the most significant details about his life is actually his death. How John the Baptist died is equally if not more a part of his legacy than anything else. John's life ended in a way that doesn't quite match the man we have esteemed to be so great. John's life ended horribly.

> When Herod Antipas, the ruler of Galilee, heard about Jesus, he said to his advisers, "This must be John the Baptist raised from the dead! That is why he

can do such miracles." For Herod had arrested and imprisoned John as a favor to his wife Herodias (the former wife of Herod's brother Philip.) John had been telling Herod, "It is against God's law for you to marry her." Herod wanted to kill John, but he was afraid of a riot because all the people believed John was a prophet. But at a birthday party for Herod, Herodia's daughter performed a dance that greatly pleased him, so he promised with a vow to give her anything she wanted. At her mother's urging, the girl said, "I want the head of John the Baptist on a tray!" Then the king regretted what he said; but because of the vow he had made in front of his guests, he issued the necessary orders. So John was beheaded in the prison, and his head was brought on a tray and given to the girl, who took it to her mother. Later John's disciples came for his body and buried it. Then they went and told Jesus what had happened.[25]

John didn't have the opportunity to choose how his life ended, although I'm almost certain he would have never chosen the ending he received. No one would have chosen for a life so brilliantly lived to end so barbarically, no matter how heroic they were. John's life was indeed an adventure and was recorded in a book, but he never had the opportunity to choose a different path for his life and death.

## Different Endings

I once heard a story about a man and his son who were sitting together watching an intense action movie. As they sat together glued to the television, the young boy's emotions became intertwined with the characters in the movie. With each twist and turn of the plot, the young boy's heart pounded with the intensity

---

[25]Matthew 14:1-12 NLT.

of the moment. His heart was attached to the hero of the film. Every climatic moment caused him to cringe with fear as he felt the gravity and weight of each scene. He was concerned about the plight of the hero. Would he survive? How would he escape from his enemies? Would he make it out alive and rescue the girl before she met her demise?

After nearly two hours of intense emotion, the movie finally wound down to its final minutes, and in the closing scene, the hero of the film found himself facing his most difficult challenge yet. The young boy felt deep within himself that this time the hero would not make it out alive. Bracing himself for the worst possible outcome, the boy turned to his left to watch his father's response to the moment. His father seemed unmoved by the moment. When the movie was over, and all was well with the hero, the young boy mentioned to his father that he noticed he was either unaware or uninterested in the possibility that the hero may not have made it through the last scene of the movie. When the young boy asked his father why he had seemed so calm during such an intense moment, the young boy's father simply replied, "Simple, son. I wasn't afraid of what would happen because I've already read the book!"

Life is full of twists and turns that cause many to question how their lives will end. In my opinion, the question of endings is one of the most essential yet ignored questions that we could and should ask of ourselves. When it comes to life, there is no book we can read to determine how it will all end. We have the benefit of reading how John's story ended, but he didn't. I would never have chosen John's fate, and you would most certainly agree that you would have never chosen that ending, either. Although I have no intention of having to face an ending quite so horrific, I have had some very painful moments in my life that did not end quite as gracefully as I would have wished, especially since I now have the benefit of reflecting on the past and its effects on my life today.

When we become concerned with the remote possibility of a difficult or dangerous ending, we become increasingly focused on changing the circumstances that we believe contribute to that ending. If I can change my circumstances, then I can change my ending. If I can change my characteristics, then perhaps I can change my character. When we want things to end differently, we tend to believe we can alter the ending by changing the narrative, oftentimes in mid-story. The most critical mistake we make is that in our effort to divert what we discern may be a difficult ending, we often deny ourselves the opportunity to live how we are designed and destined to live, no matter how different it makes us appear.

John the Baptist may not have chosen his deadly ending, but he did have a choice to not change himself. John chose not to deny himself the opportunity and experience of living the life he was destined and designed to live. John was different. He knew it, and so did everyone around him.

> In those days, John the Baptist came to the Judean wilderness and began preaching. His message was, "Repent of your sins and turn to God, for the Kingdom of Heaven is near." The prophet Isaiah was speaking about John when he said, "He is a voice shouting in the wilderness, 'Prepare the way for the Lord's coming! Clear the road for him!'" John's clothes were woven from coarse camel hair, and he wore a leather belt around his waist. For food he ate locusts and wild honey. People from Jerusalem and from all of Judea and all over the Jordan Valley went out to see and hear John.[26]

In just a few words, Matthew is able to give us a snapshot of John the Baptist, and in case you missed it, Matthew, in not so many words, tells us that John the Baptist is pretty weird. After describing John's behavior, Matthew takes the time and space to insert a description of John's wardrobe and diet into his narrative, turning our attention to something that highlights the fact that John was indeed a different kind of guy.

---

[26]Matthew 3:1-4 NLT.

It almost seems like an out of place, irrelevant piece of information. I mean, if you left out what John wore and what he ate, you could probably get a pretty decent grasp of the type of person he was. He preached a message of repentance, and Matthew even connects his audience with the prophet Isaiah, as it relates to John's identity. The idea that Matthew would take time to talk about John's clothes means that it was a subtle yet important part of John's persona. John was different.

I'm not absolutely certain about fashion trends in first-century Palestine, and I am even more uncertain about the latest fitness crazes and fad diets in Jerusalem in those days, but I am almost certain that Matthew was pointing out some pretty unorthodox behavior in the person of John the Baptist. John wore weird outfits, and he ate bugs. Now that's a different kind of guy. He draws plenty of attention to himself because he is so different. In fact, Matthew insists that people came from all over to "*see* and hear John."

John was so different that his life would demand a different type of ending, but it wasn't just John's ending that was different. His beginning was almost equally as different.

> One day Zechariah was serving God in the Temple, for his order was on duty that week. As was the custom of the priests, he was chosen by lot to enter the sanctuary of the Lord and burn incense. While the incense was being burned a great crowd stood outside praying. While Zechariah was in the sanctuary, an angel of the Lord appeared to him, standing to the right of the incense altar. Zechariah was shaken and overwhelmed with fear when he saw him. But the angel said, "Don't be afraid, Zechariah! God has heard your prayer. Your wife Elizabeth, will give you a son, and you are to name him John. You will have great joy and gladness, and

many will rejoice at his birth, for he will be great in
the eyes of the Lord." [27]

John's beginning was just as strange and different as his end.
John the Baptist was born to parents who had both passed their
childbearing years. Simply put, John's parents were extremely old.
After several years of being childless, it seemed as though they had
given up any hope of one day having children. Zechariah had
begun to reconcile with the fact that he would have no son to whom
he could pass his legacy. Elizabeth had begun to settle into the idea
that she may always be associated with her seeming inability to
have children. John's parents had long since suspended their
dreams of being parents when suddenly they got word that they
will have a son.

John's birth narrative is surrounded with details of a divine
decision to make his life different. It was even foretold that he
would do something great for God. He would bring joy not only to
his parents but also to his people. John was born to be different.
Being different was as much a part of his life as his name. It's
almost no wonder, then, why John the Baptist was such an eccentric
and exciting figure in biblical history. He was destined to be
different from the beginning. He was almost certainly destined to
die in a manner that was much different than expected. Because of
his obvious differences, he was ultimately one of the greatest
difference-makers in ancient history and in the Christian faith.
Despite the fact that John could not choose his different beginning,
and he certainly would not have chosen his very different ending, it
did not influence his determination to live differently during the in-
between time. What we can learn from John is that our inability to
control the things that make us different should never force us to
resist living differently because *sometimes we have to be willing to be
different in order to make a difference.*

---

[27]Luke 1:8-15 NLT.

Most people spend the majority of their lives avoiding being different. This is a reality. It is human nature. We avoid being different because differences normally result in division, and we do not look forward to being separated or singled out from the crowd because, quite frankly, it doesn't normally end well. At least that's what we've been told to believe.

Different does not always have to lead to division. Different doesn't always mean dysfunctional. Being different does not always mean your life will be difficult. All throughout history, people who were dramatically different led lives that had a tremendous impact in our lifetime and beyond. John was a dramatically different kind of guy who ate bugs and wore camel's hair and preached in the wilderness, yet he made such a dramatic difference in the world that his life served as the catalyst for the eventual demise of the greatest empire in the world.

It was John the Baptist who had a head-to-head encounter with King Herod, the same Herod who was a part of a dynasty complicit in establishing and maintaining Roman rule over the Jewish people. Herod Antipas was the son of Herod the Great, the same Herod the Great who once tried to kill Jesus by having all male children under the age of two murdered because he felt threatened by the announcement of a newborn king of the Jews.

One day, Herod Antipas, who had John killed, gets word about the man John came to introduce to the world. John's divine purpose in life was to point the Jewish people to Jesus. When Herod hears about all the things Jesus is doing, the only person he could compare him to was the strange bug-eating preacher named John that he had killed. John was so different that even after he died, his name became synonymous with Jesus. That Jesus that John introduced would eventually be killed, only to have a man named Paul be imprisoned and sent to Herod Agrippa, a relative of Herod's long-ruling family, for preaching about the same Jesus John introduced. It was Herod Agrippa who sent Paul to Rome, a move that would eventually make Rome the epicenter of the Christian movement. I think it's safe to say that, although John was different, it was clear he had a divine purpose. His life began in a way that he didn't choose for himself, and his life ended in a way that no one would choose, but John did choose to live his life in a way that made a tremendous difference. He made a difference because he chose to be different, and that's a choice we can all make.

## Divinely Different

I don't know how my life will end, but I have a suspicion it will be a different type of ending because of my beginning. From the beginning of my existence, I have been different. Perhaps I was born to be different, and if that's the case, then every strange and weird part of me I have tried to hide for years is actually a part of the divine DNA given to me by God. As I grew older, I began to understand that each difference and every disability I had was connected to my understanding of God.

> When it comes to suffering, I'm convinced God has more in mind for us than to simply avoid it, give it ibuprofen, divorce it, institutionalize it, or miraculously heal it. But how do we embrace that which God gives from his left hand? I have found that a person's contentment with impairment is directly proportional to the understanding of God and his Word. If a person with a disability is disappointed with God, it can usually be traced to a thin view of the God of the Bible. [28]

What we believe about our weaknesses, our differences, and our disabilities says a lot about what we really believe about God. I am quite certain that many people grew up with an extremely "thin view" of God. I will be the first to admit that despite my church background and growing up in a Christian home, I understood very little about who God was and how He actually worked. Like many people, I assumed that God was a mean old man who sat in a

---

[28]Michael S. Bates, *Disability & The Gospel*, 9.

chair somewhere in the clouds, just waiting for me to mess up so he could give me some horrible disease as his divine and just punishment for my disobedience.

The problem with this line of thinking is that when you constantly believe that God is out to get you, you will constantly feel as though God doesn't get you. God can't possibly understand my struggle if He continues to punish me for being different. In fact, if I was born with a deficiency, then how will I ever get my life together? God can't be all that concerned with my salvation if I have no way of accomplishing anything worthy of his standards.

Humanity has a long history of connecting our disabilities to God's judgment. Somewhere along the line, we began to assume that being born differently abled was a punishment for something someone had done, even though we ourselves couldn't possibly have done something to deserve such a punishment. When it's all said and done, it doesn't seem to matter much that we didn't do anything to deserve what, we feel, makes us so different. Instead, we just begin feeling guilty about it.

So why do I feel guilty most of the time? I think I feel guilty because we are all taught at a very early age that when something is "wrong" with someone, then something is not "right." In other words, someone must be right in order for someone to be wrong. When it comes to any type of developmental disability or mental or physical disability, we want to look for a cause. Someone or something must not be right because when we look at that person who is different, it is obvious that something is wrong. In John chapter 9, Jesus runs into that very issue with his disciples.

> As Jesus was walking along, he saw a man who had been blind from birth. "Rabbi," his disciples asked him, "why was this man born blind? Was it because of his own sins or his parents' sins?" "It was not because of his sins or his parents' sins," Jesus

answered. "This happened so the power of God could be seen in him."[29]

According to Jesus, the reason the man couldn't see wasn't because someone or something wasn't right. Jesus seems to suggest that the blind man could be just the right person to help others see the power of God.

Imagine God is so powerful that He works through our differences and our disabilities. Imagine a God so powerful that our limits have no authority to limit God's abilities. Imagine, if you will, a world in which God takes full responsibility for assuring that each person with a difference or disability has value and dignity because God chooses to use their difference as a platform for pointing people to himself. I believe there is no greater privilege than to be a person God can use to orchestrate his perfect plan. Although God's plan is perfect, he doesn't require the participation of perfect people. In fact, there are many times when the imperfections of humanity serve as the perfect platform for God's purpose to be discovered. Jesus transforms our understanding of disabilities when he clearly articulates that the issue is not a shortcoming on the part of the blind man or his parents, and consequently, I believe that understanding God's perspective on persons living with any type of disability or difference is extremely important.

> We must revisit our deeply ensconced cultural assumptions about what it means to be "normal" as opposed to what it might mean to live for years in a state that must be considered "brokenness." We must strive to replace wrong-headed (even if sincere) thinking in these areas with biblically based, culturally relevant, redemption-oriented understandings of people with disabilities and brokenness in the church in America.[30]

---

[29] John 9:1-3 NLT.

[30] Michael S. Bates, *Disability & The Gospel*, 19.

If there is anything I know about being different, it is that I often did not feel "normal," and I usually felt somewhat broken, but for some unknown reason, God seemed to find a way to break through my lifelong battle of brokenness and call me to something extraordinary for even a normal person, which meant for me the call was even greater.

## Daring to Be Different

When God called me to finally become more of the me he had created me to be, it set something in motion. While I didn't understand it at the time—beyond God scaring me half to death—I can now reflect on what the spark was that ignited a passion for pursuing God's plan for me, although it would not come easy.

The next few years of my college career were spent in solitude. Well, not quite but close enough. Following the major accident, and a major moment with God, I moved across the campus into a dormitory that contained only single rooms. The rooms in this dorm were extremely small. I barely had enough space for my things to fit, but I knew I needed to retreat into a space where I could begin the process of making some sense of my life. In retrospect, I was much happier living alone. Isolating myself from the crazy environment that had become my life seemed almost instinctive. It was like I thrived in the solitude of being left to myself.

My grades got better. I had several consecutive semesters of barely missing the dean's list. I miraculously relinquished my appetite for drugs and alcohol, perhaps because I no longer needed them to perform and play the role of someone else. I also seemed to be a bit more focused on my athletic career. Everything seemed to be coming together in my life. I even began to feel more spiritually satisfied. Being alone turned out to not be such a bad thing after all, even if I did have to endure the endless taunts of my teammates for living a life of solitude.

Eventually, my girlfriend, who is now my wife, began a relationship with me that met most, if not all, of my social needs. Without the drugs and alcohol helping me to create a false image, I discovered—or rediscovered—how socially awkward I was. Within a matter of months, it became obvious to some, and more obvious to others, that I was a little strange and different, but with my girlfriend, it didn't seem to matter much.

We were, and continue to be, the complete opposite of one another. She is the personification of what it means to be social. She loves to talk, and she very rarely meets a stranger. She can connect with almost anyone instantly, and that's without a doubt the most beneficial characteristic of her personality because it helped her to connect with me. I am not a social butterfly, and when my drinking days ended, I realized I had plenty of friendships but no real relationships.

I quickly learned that she was as brilliant as she was beautiful. As a foreign student, she came to the United States from Malawi, Africa, to attend college at the age of sixteen. Although I was a pretty decent student at this point, I had spent so many years pretending to be someone I wasn't that I wasn't sure I was smart enough for her. She was driven and dedicated. She knew what she wanted, and it was obvious that she was a leader and looking to live out her dreams. It was almost as though when God allowed me to cross her path, I was finally confronted with an example of what it would look like to be a person who was completely comfortable in the skin God had blessed them with. For the first time, I had an up-close glimpse of someone who wasn't trying to be someone else. For the first time, I was confronted with my own mistake. This was what life was supposed to look like when it was totally authentic.

It didn't take long until she had my heart. Growing up, I didn't have a lot of relationships, especially with girls. Don't get me wrong—I had a few girlfriends, but I can now honestly say that none of those relationships would have led to anything substantial because those girls were never dating the real me. They were dating someone I created. This time around, though, I had found someone who would finally get a chance to find out who I really was, and in the process, I would begin to find out who I was, too.

Once we started officially dating, we became almost inseparable. It was a good thing, too, because having a real relationship with someone who saw past my quirks and differences helped me learn to let my guard down and be more of myself. In the past, I had experienced so many negative reactions to the way I behaved that I had learned to adjust my behavior to whomever I was dealing with at the time. I had become good at being a good enough person for everyone else except me. God knows I was exhausted, and if I was going to develop any meaningful relationships, it was going to require me to learn that being good for everyone else wasn't exactly good for me. With Isabella, I didn't have to just be good for her — she was also interested in me being good for me.

After a year of dating, I knew that I wanted to stick together, permanently. At this point, I didn't have a ton of experience in romantic love. Honestly, I had none, so the question of love wasn't clearly defined for me. I knew I loved her in the sense that I had no other person to compare her to. What I felt was totally new and totally important to me. Being socially awkward meant that I was bound to blow it at some point; I always did. I could never quite explain what went wrong with other people I tried to connect with, but it was apparent that the problem was me. That didn't happen this time. I think I was learning what love was, and not just from another person — with her, I was learning what divine love was. I was learning how love can and will make you more of who you are at the same time it is moving toward the best version of who you can be.

I loved her, and it was a God thing, so I knew this relationship had to be made permanent. Isabella was a year ahead of me in school, so she was preparing to graduate, while I still had a whole other year of school to complete. I had no real money, and no real plan, but I knew she had my heart permanently. She had seen a glimpse of the real me — the awkward, weird, difficult to get along with, strange, differently abled person who had no idea what was wrong with himself—and she didn't bail out on me, so she had my real heart forever.

You can already gather the happy ending to this love story. I proposed to her, she said yes of course, and despite spending a year apart while I completed my undergraduate education, we stuck together. We are still together, and today we have three beautiful boys. While our relationship wasn't always easy, I do know now what love looks life through how we have had to constantly adjust to the curve balls that life kept throwing at us. One such curve ball came approximately a year into our young marriage when I felt that God was calling me to become a pastor.

After graduating from college, Isabella moved to the Atlanta area where she had family. She lived with her relatives until she was stable enough to find gainful employment. Naturally, once I graduated, I also moved to Atlanta. Isabella had already found a church she enjoyed attending, and because it was a church she loved, I joined her there. Six months after I arrived in Atlanta, we were married.

We were enjoying life together as a young newly married couple. We loved our church, and we were becoming more actively involved in volunteering. I was becoming more involved in a ministry for young adults ages twenty-one to thirty-five. I'm not sure when it happened, but I started to change. This time, the changes I was making weren't driven by a need to be different. I can't exactly pinpoint the date or the time, but what I can recall is that I felt as though my life was becoming better, not perfect but better than I believed it could be.

We married in January of 2001, and by November of the same year, I had an experience that changed my life. My relationship with God changed dramatically at the age of twenty-three. I was still quite young. I hadn't even been married a full year. I was beginning to learn how to become more of myself, and that was wonderful, yet God seemed to want to pull even more out of me. It seemed as though he had placed me in the right relationship and in the right mental and emotional state to get me to this one moment in life that would deepen my personal spiritual journey. One night, in a very vivid dream, I felt God call me into a life of service to him as a pastor.

My wife seemed to be unsurprised yet equally as terrified as I was. I can recall spending nearly the entire next year of my life wrestling with what I knew God was inviting me to become. Just when I had begun the process of familiarizing myself with me, God reached inside my chest and pulled my heart right out. That's what it felt like. It literally felt like one of the most painful experiences I have ever had to that day. God wanted to put me out there. No, God actually wanted to *push* me out there, way beyond my comfort zone and far beyond my natural capabilities, and it felt like I was being punished for being me. It felt like one cruel commandment, and I kept this communication from God to myself for as long as I possibly could, hoping and praying I was completely wrong about what I had discerned.

After about a year of hiding and running, the burden to obey became unbearable. I was still not happy about it. Pastors have to stand up in front of people and talk. That was not something that I was even remotely interested in doing. I didn't have anything to say, and more importantly, no one would want to hear from a weird freak like me. I didn't even get along with most people most of the time. I didn't understand people, and I still didn't fully understand myself. Going to church was one thing; leading a church was an entirely different type of life that on the surface did not seem very logical or fair to ask someone like me to do.

In many ways, the news felt like a setback. As a result, I spent a significant amount of time in hiding. I once again felt the need to hide something about myself, except this time it was the part of me that was giving me the most relief, my faith. For almost a year, I wrestled with even letting people at work know I was a Christian because I couldn't handle the expectations of again having to be someone I wasn't. To me, Christians, especially pastors, were good people, perfect people even. I was still broken. I still was so far from accepting myself that I just couldn't accept being asked to be someone else again.

Fortunately for me, following God is always a process. My process took a little over a year, but I was finally ready to admit that becoming more of the me God created me to be came at the cost becoming what God was calling me to be. Eventually, I learned that these two ideas are not mutually exclusive. If I was going to be different, then that meant I was going to have to believe differently, especially when it came to serving God with my life.

A large part of me failed to understand that I wasn't being compelled to change who I was to serve God. I am almost certain that serving him in the capacity to which I was being called served to further free me from the bondage of believing I was intentionally created as an inferior product and person. Pastor and author John Piper writes:

> It would reflect a theological prejudice to deny that the author means man's physical appearance images his Maker. As von Rad says, "Man's bodily appearance is not at all to be excepted from the realm of God's image…" Therefore, one will do well to split the physical from the spiritual as little as possible: the whole human man is created in God's image.[31]

Serving God as a pastor communicated something about God's expectation that nothing God creates is so different or disabled that it lacks the ability to be connected to God through lifelong service. Learning to live with this was a challenge, but it was a challenge I wanted and needed to embrace. My journey began with my wife by my side. Over the years, we would serve many churches, one of which we helped plant in 2007. We learned several lessons along the way, but it would be several years into pursuing my calling that

---

[31] Nancy Eiesland, *The Disabled God: Toward a Liberatory Theology of Disability*, 20.

I would finally get the critical answers to the questions I always had about who I was and why I behaved the way I did.

In 2010, after several years of living in the Atlanta area, my family moved to Lagrange, GA. I knew very little about Lagrange except that it was about sixty miles south of Atlanta. New Community Church was looking for a youth pastor, and for some strange reason, I felt compelled to apply for the position. During this time, I was serving as both a hospice chaplain and a pastor. The small church we planted in Dallas, GA was an unpaid position, so my income came from chaplaincy. While I enjoyed the ministry of chaplaincy, my heart was being directed toward working in the church on a full-time basis. Although the conversation with our church leadership was tough, it was honest and loving, and we both agreed that following God's plan for my life required me to explore where God may be trying to send me.

By the end of June of 2010, New Community Church had offered me the position. I agreed to join their pastoral team, but the reality that I had to change jobs, change churches, and change cities almost made me come unglued. I didn't do change very well. We had lived in the same area for nearly ten years. Making a move of this magnitude was certainly not my preference, especially since it ultimately meant having to surround myself with a new group of people. I was deathly afraid of making the move, and the reality is it was nearly a year into our transition before I stopped questioning whether or not I had made the right decision.

The transition to Lagrange was actually very smooth. The pastor and leadership of the church treated us very well, but the terror didn't go away. I felt like a fish out of water. On the outside, I think I was able to hold it together just enough to make people believe I was confident in our choice to join this wonderful church, but inside I was struggling. Just one month into our transition into the community, my father-in-law died suddenly in Malawi. I had to put my wife on a plane with her mother, who was visiting with us at the time, and send them back home to Malawi to bury their husband and father. Left behind with two small children for nearly three weeks, I went into a deep depression. I was certain that I was not going to survive this move and all the circumstances that surrounded it.

The entire first month of our move set something in motion that was extremely terrifying for me. I began to experience physical symptoms I had never experienced before. I was near a complete physical and mental collapse, and although grief was a contributing factor, I knew that something else was going on. On a random morning of doing my daily routine of getting our two boys ready for school, I collapsed in our bathroom. Fortunately, I came to without any injuries or further incidents, but the incident did lead me to seek medical attention for an explanation to this strange episode. Strapped with a heart monitor for an entire week, I was monitored to assess the source of my issues, to no avail. After a battery of tests, my doctor was unable to find anything physically wrong with me. We instead assumed and agreed that it was due to the significant amount of stress that I was under.

I knew better, though, and I knew that somehow it had everything to do with the same reasons I had pretended to be someone I wasn't for years. I knew that this "thing" I had been dealing with for years was still very much an issue, and it was most likely due to being thrust into an entirely new city and setting, and I was completely overwhelmed and in over my head. Unfortunately for me, it wouldn't be the last time.

# CHAPTER 5
# I AM SEARCHING

## Tangled

The next year would find me being stretched in ways I could have never have imagined. My life was quickly turning into a tangled mess of mental and emotional knots. After spending nearly eleven years in the Atlanta area and spending over three years as a hospice chaplain and pastor of a small church, I discovered that I was completely comfortable in those two settings. Adjusting to life in a new city and church was really hard on me, but I learned to fake it as much as I could and as much as I had to.

Being the youth pastor did have its advantages. My position didn't require me to spend much time around adults. Except for the dedicated adults who served as our volunteers, I spent most of my time around teenagers, and since most teenagers are as socially awkward as I am, I was able to manage socially. My time spent serving the teens of our church was actually transformative for me. I was blessed with the opportunity to learn how to interact with people socially in a new setting, and the fact that I wasn't pressured to meet certain social expectations helped me gain confidence.

While I was gaining confidence in my social skills, it would still take me about two years to become completely comfortable. I did have a few awkward moments, mostly with adults, but my exposure to the adult population of the church was so limited that it did not prevent me from doing a fairly good job at creating a healthy, growing, and exciting youth program at our church. I was excited about the progress we were making, but more importantly, I was excited that I was actually starting to fit in. In fact, I was so excited that I began to explore options for pursuing my doctorate degree. For the first time since my call to become a pastor, I felt that I could actually succeed at this profession despite my secret social anxiety.

In January of 2012, I began pursuing my doctorate. I was establishing a new routine, and it was working well for me. I was slowly reaching a level of confidence in who I was and what my role was at the church, and then suddenly, after one semester of school and after two years of learning to get comfortable with my role at New Community Church, life changed instantly. The summer of 2012 brought the greatest challenge I would ever face in my entire adult life. A few weeks after my thirty-fourth birthday, I tore my right Achilles tendon while playing basketball with a few of the guys from our church youth group. The extent of my injury would require surgery and nearly a year of recovery time, but what happened after that would prove to be a much tougher situation for me to overcome.

One August afternoon, while sitting in my recliner reading and writing papers for class and taking medications needed for my post-op recovery, I received a message that an emergency staff meeting was being called for the next day. Immediately, I panicked. I wasn't quite sure what the meeting was about, and that made me anxious. I was really disconnected from the church because I had spent the majority of my summer trying to recover from surgery.

The next day, a coworker picked me up and escorted me to the church for the emergency meeting. What I remember most about the day was that the room was tense. I'm fairly sure that everyone shared in my anxiety, perhaps for different reasons, but the anxiety was the same. After we waited apprehensively, the pastor entered the room, greeted us all, and sat down. The news was just as we had all suspected. Effective immediately, he was resigning as the pastor of the church.

My heart was broken. He had brought me onto the staff at the church because he saw something in me that I probably didn't even see in myself at the time. The news was definitely not something I wanted to hear, but honestly, I was anxious because the thought of having to work for someone else caused me to panic. It had taken me two years to adjust to my new surroundings and new coworkers, and with one simple statement, my sense of security was set back ten years. I was a wreck, and my first and most natural thought was to run away from the problem because there was no way I was going to go through having to do it all over again.

Over the next several months, I struggled silently with mild depression. I say it was mild, but between the news of having a significant change in my work environment and the ongoing recovery from a major surgery, I was probably more depressed than I would like to have admitted. Even now as I reflect back to those dark days, I can recall serious changes in my attitude, my appetite, and my sleep pattern. I wasn't myself, and because life had taught me how to pretend so well at being someone else, no one really knew the extent to which I was affected by this situation.

Initially, the only thing that stopped me from exiting the church quietly was my immense fear of starting over again somewhere else. There was a very clear possibility of having to start over where I was, but when I weighed it against quitting the church and possibly going through the process of finding another place to work and worship and the possibility of moving my family again along with the possibility of having to meet an entirely new set of people with an entirely new set of standards, I was simply too afraid to leave. Starting over again at my current church was the lesser of two evils in my eyes, and I had grown to accept that as my fate—until I was inspired to view things differently.

I've always been introverted, and because I don't particularly feel the need to draw attention to myself, it could also be said that it takes a lot to gain my attention as well. Perhaps that's why certain images and symbols capture my attention more readily than others. There are just some images that are so significant to the way I process things in my mind that they have become synonymous with my faith. No time is this truer for me than when I have a significant and memorable dream that captivates my imagination while communicating a critical message.

Approximately six weeks after the pastor resigned from our church, I had a dream. This dream was a clear and convincing message. I didn't have these types of dreams often. I had had this type of experience only two other times. On both occasions, a clear message was communicated to me, using a person who appeared in my dreams as a symbolic messenger who was synonymous with a divine message from God. For some reason, this night he brought with him a message that terrified me to my core. The message was clear: God wanted me to submit my application to the committee who would be searching for the new pastor of our church.

My first thought was how ridiculous that sounded, especially since they had yet to even announce what the plan was for replacing the pastor. My second thought was that there was no way I was ready or willing to take on the challenge of having to lead a church with the expectations I assumed people would have of me as their pastor. I had barely reached the point of being able to socially interact with the parents of the youth program I was managing. There was no way I could do any more than that. At that point, my faith had taken a turn for the worse. God was out of his mind if he thought I was going to do that. Not going to happen. No way, no how—or so I thought.

God is so much smarter than we are. It is a realization that I continue to be confronted with on almost a daily basis, and on this occasion, I was given a harsh reminder that I was not nearly as smart as I thought I was. I was determined to disregard what I knew to be a clear expectation that God had of me. I didn't want to pastor. Well, I did want to pastor someday and somewhere, but I just wasn't sure that this was the circumstance by which I wanted that dream to happen. Truthfully, I was afraid, and it was not just a nervous anxiety type of fear. It was a kind of fear so deep-seated that I realized I was far too weak as a person to lead a group of people on a journey that I was still trying to navigate myself.

Over the next sixteen months, the church went through a transition process as it sought out its next leader. During that time frame, I functioned in a variety of roles, one of which included a more visible role in the adult worship services. I had to do more speaking in the adult services, which meant I had to do more interacting with the adult population of our church. Each week was more terrifying than the week before. Working with teens was much easier and much more comfortable, and I had learned how to survive in that setting, but surrounding myself with adults led to a totally new set of social expectations. Expectations that I honestly did not know even existed.

The entire sixteen-month transition left me completely exposed. The state of my emotional and mental health was tantamount to a fish struggling to survive out of water. It was hard for me to breathe emotionally, spiritually, mentally, socially, and yes, even literally. Unbeknownst to many people around me, I had begun having frequent and severe panic attacks. Every week, I would mount the stage to give a message to a room full of people who literally took my breath away. It was a painful and draining time, not just emotionally, but physically as well.

Around this time, I was taking a course in a doctorate program that was designed to help pastors explore themselves more intimately. As a part of this course, I was required to have six people that I work with complete an evaluation of their observations of me as a leader and a person. Obviously, these types of exercises can yield very little results depending on the evaluator's candor and honesty, and for the most part, the feedback I received was all positive except for one evaluation from someone I held in high regard and trusted immensely. It exposed me to some characteristics I had no awareness of. In his evaluation, he noted that I managed social relationships well in a small group, but when in a larger group, I tended to miss social cues.

I had never heard myself described in those terms before. Actually, I did not even know what a "social cue" was. What I was starting to realize was that I was being exposed to an entirely new way to understand myself, and all of it, quite honestly, was not easy to accept. It wasn't just the evaluation that pushed me in the direction of self-discovery. The entire leadership transition and pastoral search was successful in pushing me to the edge of my limitations, and at the edge was a gigantic mirror that exposed me to who I really was.

Although I grew up hearing some pretty strange and sometimes offensive comments about my personality, I had never truly been exposed to the untethered raw and honest feedback and criticism I experienced as a result of being a visible presence in the church and a candidate to potentially become its next leader. There was something about the entire scenario that slowly wore me down to the point of complete mental, physical, and emotional exhaustion, and it was in that place where the real me begin to peek through. I was no longer able to adapt and adjust to my surroundings and my new social settings because I didn't have the time to study the context and master the art of mimicking "acceptable" behavior.

Adult church was louder than youth ministry. Some people were more aggressive socially. I wasn't allowed much space to process. The game and its rules had totally changed while I was playing in it, and I was falling behind the count because when it came to my ability to handle myself socially, I was striking out and striking out horribly. What was supposed to be a "calling" from God, or so I thought, ended up feeling like a sixteen-month audition, an audition that would rival the likes of reality TV shows like *The Apprentice* and *Hell's Kitchen*. The lights and cameras were indeed on me, and there was plenty of unwanted action going on.

The biggest complaints and critiques that I heard—both formally and informally—had nothing to do with my competence or my communication abilities from the stage. Most if not all negative feedback had to do with what many people felt were character flaws. I was too introverted. I didn't speak to people. I never stayed after service to shake hands with the congregation. I was even accused of walking right past someone who wanted to speak to me and ignoring her as if she were unimportant and insignificant. The problem is I never felt as though I did any of those things. I certainly did not feel I was the type of person who rejected the idea of embracing people openly.

At first, I became defensive. I mean really defensive. I made it my mission to defend my character and my reputation. I was not "too" introverted. I was a people person. I did love people, and I could shake hands and be social as much as the last pastor, but I wasn't going to do it with a bunch of people who assumed that they had no responsibility to be civil to me. I deserved to be treated fairly, too, and I just didn't want to believe that people could actually think that I was that type of person. The problem I kept running into when I rehearsed my argument in my mind was I couldn't figure out why it was necessary for so many people to insist that I was that type of person. It wasn't making sense to me, and the only thing I could do was eventually come to grips with the fact that perhaps there was some truth to what was being said, and I had to find out why.

## Untying the Knots

A few years ago, when our middle child was around two years old, I noticed a new strange behavior. On occasion, I would see him in his room fumbling around with his brother's shoes. After several minutes of tossing them back and forth, he would proceed to go into a full emotional meltdown. He would scream at the top of his lungs and toss the shoes into the corner of the room with all the strength his little two-year-old arms could muster.

At first, it was amusing, and then after witnessing it happen on a few more occasions, it became puzzling. After a few days of this behavior, it became annoying and downright disturbing. I couldn't figure out for the life of me what the problem was. He didn't seem to be hurt or in any type of pain, and he definitely wasn't in any danger. He wasn't able to articulate why he was so angry and frustrated, and I wasn't sure what to do or how to handle it.

Then one day it dawned on me that his fixation with his brother's shoes was based on his need to go somewhere. He didn't want to go anywhere in particular—he just wanted to go. The shoes symbolized progress, movement, adventure, and independence. He wanted to go somewhere, and getting shoes on was the first step in being able to explore places that he imagined were outside the door of our tiny apartment.

The frustration came in when he was unable to put the shoes on properly because they were tied in knots. Now, on almost every occasion that he had these meltdowns, we had no plans to leave the house. Most of his frustration wasn't based on the reality of everyone else in the house; it was based on his own separate and unique view of the world around him. Whether we were actually planning to leave the house or not was the least of his concerns. His issue was that without being able to put the shoes on, he would never be able to go anywhere, and his frustration was that the knots in his shoes prevented the possibility of him ever moving beyond where he currently was.

Nearly halfway through the sixteen-month leadership transition at New Community Church, I began to realize three critical realities that I knew I would have to eventually confront. First, I was operating on a reality that was completely different than those around me. The comments and observations that people had of me clearly exposed a discrepancy between my world and their world, and while I wasn't quite ready to concede that I was wrong, I was at least beginning to entertain the idea that my entire outlook on life was different than most.

Second, my entire life was in knots. My emotions, ideas, self-image, self-esteem, and social intelligence was completely tangled into a ball of complicated humanity that was so complex it resembled a set of old Christmas tree lights that were not stored away properly. My life was a mess, and it took me being pushed to the head of the class to find out how much of a tangled knotted up mess my life was. I knew so little about who I was, and it took others to subtly point me in the direction of finding out more.

Finally, and most importantly, I realized that if I was ever going to go anywhere in life, I was going to have to get help with untying the ugly knots that prevented me from putting on my shoes and stepping into a new role in life and a new role in our church. God was ready to give me the shoes. I just had to admit that I wasn't ready to put them on, at least not until I was willing to admit they were all knotted up.

By the time I had reached this stage, I knew that the issue was never going to be about whether or not I was going to be the next pastor of New Community Church, or if I was even competent enough to be the next pastor. The issue I was forced to face was the need to look inward. The late Dag Hammarskjold, once the secretary-general of the United Nations, suggested that we have become adept at exploring outer space, but we have not developed similar skills in exploring our own personal inner spaces. He wrote, "The longest journey of any person is the journey inward." [32]

Most people are subconsciously afraid of digging too deep. Our culture has taught us to remain superficial. We live in a highly extroverted culture, particularly in the west. We learn who we are by what we earn, what we wear, where we live, and the places we frequent. It's no wonder why almost all of the ways that we choose to identify ourselves are superficial and surface. I had to admit that even though I had done some of the work in not pretending to be someone that I wasn't, like an iceberg floating in the arctic, I had much more lying beneath the surface that I had failed to address.

I needed the language to articulate what my experience in everyday life was like. As I mentioned earlier, I had taken a course in my- doctorate program that required the use of a number of personality assessments. One of those assessments was the Myers-Briggs Personality Type assessment. According to the Myers-Briggs, I was an INTJ (introversion, intuition, thinking, judgment). If you're unfamiliar with this assessment, it is an excellent tool for gaining insight into your personality type. In many cases, you can find a free Myers-Briggs assessment online, and get your results immediately after taking the assessment. The assessment will

---

[32] Peter Scazzero, *The Emotionally Healthy Church*, 75.

assign you any combination of four letters that are designed to help you understand your personality better.

I fully recommend that you take the assessment if you have not already. If nothing else, it will help you to untie your own knots. As for me, I didn't understand all the complexities of my personality at the time, but the one striking insight was my discovery of the concept of introversion. I am an introvert. That seemed to fit me very well. I wasn't a very active or proactive person when it came to social interaction. I had an extremely high value for periods of solitude. I often felt drained and overwhelmed by large crowds and felt energized by spending time alone. I was definitely more of a thinker than a talker. After reading more and more about the characteristics of introverts, I figured I had discovered the term that defined my view of the world. All I had to do was learn more about my personality type, and then I could consider my knots untied. I would be ready to move on with my life.

Unfortunately, none of that happened. Over the next few months, I would continue to struggle. As the months progressed, I became more and more of the primary leader and point of contact for all decisions made at the church during the pastor search. On the outside, I was managing, but on the inside, I had no real answers as to why I continued to feel like a fish out of water who couldn't untie his knotted shoes. I think a large part of my stalled progress in going beneath the surface happened when I began to observe other introverts. There were some definite similarities, but the more I studied the personality type and the more self-aware I became, I realized that my struggles and my issues extended far beyond the boundaries of introversion.

Ways of thinking and lifelong habits became more pronounced, or at least I became more aware of the way I thought and behaved. I began to take full notice of the things that scared me and the situations that frustrated me and the moments I walked away from an encounter confused. I paid close attention to the disagreements and arguments I had with people close to me. I made a record of my encounters with my wife and would use those moments of contention to ask myself some tough questions. Why was I so frustrated by that? What am I not understanding about what happened yesterday? Why does she think I'm angry, sad, or disinterested?

For about three months straight, I monitored my relationships, and finally, I came full circle back to conversations and interactions I had with people before and during the leadership transition at our church. I began to place the comments about me into categories, and what I discovered is that there were a number of credible complaints about my interpersonal communication skills, my demeanor and facial expressions, and my overall ability to read a person's body language. I even begin to discover that I was not all that great at picking up on sarcasm and other comments and jokes that involved discerning meaning through voice inflection and intonation.

What happened next was probably more of an act of God than I realized at the time. I felt compelled to dig for a diagnosis to what I was experiencing. Armed with this newfound understanding of what people actually thought of me and the stories and memories of my painful past as a child who couldn't quite connect with children my age, I went to credible Internet sources, books, articles, and other literature and compiled my information to see what I could possibly diagnose myself with. After a few weeks of research, watching videos, and reading, I came across a description that I thought fit me more accurately than the introvert label. That was when I was introduced to Asperger's syndrome.

I'm not sure what I was really expecting to discover about myself. I knew I wanted answers, but I'm not sure I was quite prepared for what my quest for self-discovery would eventually lead to. Until this point, I knew very little about Asperger's syndrome. I had known of only one other person who was diagnosed with it, and he was a young boy who at first glance didn't seem to have any severe disabilities. It became obvious to me that I was totally uneducated about AS. I'd heard that it was a form of autism, and then on the other hand, I had read that it was a different diagnosis altogether. I didn't know much about it, but what I did know was that almost every single key indicator associated with a confirmed diagnosis of Asperger's syndrome described my secret lifelong struggle almost perfectly. For the first time in my lifetime, I was able to clearly recognize my behavior and my struggle because I had stumbled upon the words to define my deficiencies.

Instinctively, I knew this was the truth about me. I knew I was the person described by these traits and characteristics I was reading about. I was convinced that this was what I was dealing with, but even though I was completely convinced, I remained quiet. At this point, I had not even approached my wife about my suspicions. I was silent on the matter for several months, and while I kept my newfound discovery to myself, I continued to dig deeper and deeper. It wasn't enough to read about the disorder. I wanted to hear about it as well.

The Internet became my greatest source for searching for video and audio testimonials about Asperger's syndrome. At first, I wasn't quite sure what I was looking for. In fact, I was convinced that there wasn't going to be much information available on the subject. I was wrong. I quickly discovered an entire community of people who called themselves "Aspies," a community of adults and young adults just like me, except they all seemed to be really comfortable with who they were. Many of them were extremely proud to identify themselves as such. I had stumbled into a movement, a community of people who embraced their differences and used them as a platform to share their stories and their struggles and, most of all, their successes in living and thriving with Asperger's syndrome.

I was totally amazed at the world I had just peeked into. There were so many different types of people who willingly shared their lives. So many successful, intelligent, articulate people who, like me, struggled with social interaction, and yet they all seemed to be amazingly gifted people in their own unique ways. The next several months would find me watching video after video, reading blog after blog, and doing more and more research as I uncovered a variety of ways that people were impacted by Asperger's syndrome. One day, while watching a video on YouTube, I ran across a person who would change the trajectory of my quest for understanding and encouragement in dealing with my newly defined reality. I had never even heard of Temple Grandin before, but learning about her story would change my life, to say the least.

By this time in my life, the search process at my church had been completed. In November of 2013, I had been notified that I was one of the top candidates that the elders were considering for the lead pastor job at New Community Church. I was scheduled for an interview, and just a few weeks after the interview, I was informed that the church would offer me the role of lead pastor at New Community Church effective January 1, 2014. I was excited about the opportunity, but at the same time, I was secretly scared because the process I had just gone through had exposed me to myself in a way I knew I would eventually have to expose to them, and maybe even the rest of my church.

I accepted the position, and all was well on the surface. Our church was moving forward. The people seemed happy and excited, and I was excited for them. I was doing well in my doctoral studies and was entering the final stages and planning to write my dissertation. On the surface, I was doing well, and life was moving in a new direction, but beneath the surface, I was heading in a life-altering direction. I was seriously contemplating pursuing an official diagnosis, but I knew that once I took that step, my suspicion would be confirmed and my life would become more complicated.

Before I was willing to plunge into the process of getting diagnosed, I wanted to find the most relatable cases of AS that I could find. After all, I was now the pastor of a large church, I was completing a doctorate degree, I was married with three children, and I seemed to be fairly successful. How could I be sure if there was really something going on with me when most people would likely disregard my claims because of my perceived success? I needed to see if there was anyone else who had managed to successfully navigate their social deficiencies and experienced some significant achievements in life.

Temple Grandin became a fixture of hope for me in that regard. Temple is perhaps one of the most well-known persons with autism spectrum disorder. She is an accomplished author, an educator with a Ph.D. in animal science, and she is an advocate of ASD. I had never heard of her incredible story before, but the more I dug, the more video lectures, TED talks, and books I discovered about her. She is an extremely successful, extraordinary individual who is autistic.

I soon discovered that Asperger's syndrome was not just a sub-type of autism, but it, in fact, was autism. What was once a separate explanation for what I assumed I had was now a part of a much larger understanding of a disorder. I was beginning to acknowledge the wide range of ways that people like me are affected with autism. In the world of autistic spectrum disorders, Temple, much like myself, is considered to be "high-functioning." This means that many people who are autistic are not as severely limited by their autism as others on the spectrum, but it does not mean that they are not affected at all. People like Temple Grandin are great examples of those who have maximized their abilities to reach their greatest potential in life.

By the fall of 2014, I had become quite the "expert" on Autism Spectrum Disorders. I had read so much material and had soaked in as many lectures on the subject as I could possibly stand. Armed with all this information, I knew it was time to move forward and pursue an official diagnosis, so I began by utilizing some of the great free resources available online. To my surprise, my months of research unearthed some hidden gems in the world of autism diagnosis. There were a number of websites that provided free diagnostic tools that could help people determine whether or not they were likely on the autism spectrum.

Many of the available tools are sure to provide disclaimers that they are not designed to provide an official diagnosis; however, I have found them to be extremely accurate. I tried a variety of online assessments, each time yielding a result that concluded it was "highly likely" I was on the autism spectrum. One of the best available tools was the Autism Spectrum Quotient published by Simon Baron-Cohen and his associates. I found it to be extremely insightful. I took the assessment at least three times, hoping it would be consistent so that I would be sure I was correct in my assumptions.

As it turned out, I was correct on all fronts. I even took an assessment designed to test my knowledge of facial expressions and body language, and I received a score that indicated I struggled greatly in this area. Although this was a surprise to me, I had reconciled myself with the idea that it was an experience that exposed me to some potential issues I have had in the past with understanding people and their motives and words. If nothing else, it made me rethink how I have been interacting with people my entire life.

Of all the people I regularly interact with who had been exposed to my social ineptness, my wife Isabella was the most affected. Without having an official diagnosis under my belt, I had already begun examining ways I probably had not been able to communicate effectively with her in the past. We had been married nearly fifteen years and had been in a relationship for almost four years prior to that. She knew me inside and out, and it was time to discuss my discovery with her.

## Turning on the Blue Light

I'm not sure exactly when or how I brought the subject of autism up with my wife. I can remember being nervous about discussing a topic as serious and somewhat controversial as autism. My wife had a career in working with studies on autism in children, and I wondered if perhaps I was overreacting and overreaching in my assumptions about my behavior. I had never been so nervous about having a conversation with my wife, and for some reason, I was almost afraid to bring it up. I knew, however, that if I was correct in what I was feeling, she could help me find someone who could give me an official diagnosis. When I finally got up the courage to talk to her, it was the most liberating conversation I had ever had. After months of doing my own research and having my own internal dialogue, I took the first step toward turning on the light by talking about it for the first time.

To say I was relieved would be a gross understatement. I was finally able to get outside of my own head and articulate my world in such a way that it drew my wife into my head. At first, she seemed to struggle with the idea that I may be on to something. My perception was that she was so close to me that she couldn't see the traits and behaviors that would indicate I may be a high-functioning autistic. I guess you can describe that as the beauty of our relationship—she was able to totally look past some of my shortcomings that may very well be annoying and offensive to others.

Needless to say, she was shocked but supportive. The light seemed to grow brighter as we continued to deliberate. It's amazing how much clarity can come when we process our struggles in community. The best part of talking with my wife was that I was able to hear myself talk about myself. I was beginning to understand myself in a whole new way, and for the first time ever, I heard what I sounded like. I heard not just the tone and pitch of my voice, but also the tone and pitch of my thoughts. I was learning what it was like to communicate with me, and we discovered and decided together that I needed to pursue a diagnosis. After a few weeks of searching for a clinical psychiatrist, we finally settled on one who was available to see us right away.

Prior to our initial visit, we were each tasked to complete a few assessments that the doctor forwarded to us in the mail. The assessments seemed very similar to many of the those I had already taken online. I even recognized some of the questions. My wife, however, was taking the assessments for the first time, and her task was to answer the questions based on her observations of my behavior. Overall, the evaluation would take two sessions to complete, and that made me a little anxious.

When we arrived at the appointment, I started to have feelings of deep regret. I wasn't sure I wanted to follow through with it. After all, ignorance is bliss, or so they say. Part of my anxiety stemmed from not knowing whether my suspicion would be validated. I didn't want to waste the doctor's time, and I certainly did not want to feel like a fool for making up a diagnosis that didn't exist. Before we entered the building, I took a deep breath and tried to calm myself down.

The best word to describe the first session is sterile. It felt clinical, and while I was not sure what to expect, I didn't expect it to feel the way it did. It was very scientific and structured. We talked and discussed the assessment, and she asked my wife and I some questions. In what felt like a short amount of time, it was over, and we were scheduling our next session to review her findings. The ride home was extremely long. I had too much time to think, and it was causing me to become more and more anxious. I wanted the results so that I could finally move on, but we had to wait nearly two weeks before our next scheduled appointment. Thankfully, it was December and holiday activities were ramping up at home and at my church, so my busy schedule helped to ease my anxiety somewhat.

On the day of our follow up appointment, I can remember my anxiety being at an all-time high. My life was hanging in the balance. A confirmed diagnosis would be a relief, but it would also mean a total reorientation of life. The anticipation was nauseating, and I'm certain that my behavior due to my anxiety and my obsession with the results was driving my wife crazy. It sounds completely crazy, but I actually wanted to be diagnosed. I needed validation that I wasn't intentionally reclusive, rude, and resistant to change. I needed to know that I was strange for a reason.

It was only a few days before Christmas of 2014, and not only did I get the answer that I was looking for, but I received the gift I needed. My suspicion was confirmed, and I was diagnosed with autism spectrum disorder. The blue light was finally turned on. Like a spotlight highlighting a performer on a stage, I was under the light. I was exposed, and I was exhausted. It was as though I had finally crossed the finish line, and the prize I received was learning that I wasn't "weird." I learned that when it came to certain areas of my life, I was just weak, but I could learn how to be strong.

# CHAPTER 6
# I AM WEAK

## Autism Spectrum Disorders

My life changed with this news, and though I was expecting it, I didn't know quite how to handle it. I was beginning to understand some of the many ways that I felt weak and overwhelmed in many areas of my life. I was beginning to understand why I struggled with communicating thoughts and why I was often misunderstood. I was beginning to understand why I preferred to be alone and why I preferred books over conversation. I was beginning to understand myself in a new way, but the reality was that I didn't understand autism all that well, and if I didn't understand it, then how was I supposed to explain how autism affects me to my friends, family, my staff, and my congregation? My first step in educating others had to be first educating myself.

Autism is a developmental disability and not a mental illness. In my quest to understand more about my diagnosis, I discovered that engaging the concept of understanding autism spectrum disorders is dealing with the most obvious reality that being on the spectrum may not be obvious to everyone around you.

> Diagnoses for diseases such as tuberculosis or cancer are precise. Lab tests can tell you the exact types of disease you have. Unfortunately, a diagnosis for autism, Asperger's syndrome or PDD-NOS (pervasive developmental disorder, not otherwise specified) lacks the precision of medical tests for cancer. There are no lab tests or brain scans that can be used to definitively diagnose autism spectrum disorders.[33]

---

[33] Temple Grandin, *The Way I See It.*

Autism is a spectrum. At one end of that spectrum are those who are severely affected by their autism. At the other end of the spectrum are those who are not. Individuals on the spectrum range from those who are nonverbal all the way up to those who are verbal but lack adequate social skills. While I fall on the more functional end of the spectrum, there are quite a few characteristics of autism spectrum disorder that affect me in various areas of my life.

One of the most significant discoveries for me was the idea that my brain processes the world much differently than other people. It appears that the brains of people on the autism spectrum are wired much differently than people not on the spectrum. "All minds on the autism/Asperger's spectrum are detail-oriented, but how they specialize varies."[34] I never really considered that the differences I had with others was a matter of my mind and not my personality. Unfortunately, in a highly extroverted society, personality is what we most often point to in an effort to label someone who is different. We tend to believe there are general standards for how to socially engage with others, and those standards are usually based on an assumption about what type of personality makes someone a "people person."

When I was diagnosed and began to read and learn more about autism spectrum disorders, I soon discovered that my view of the world was much different than I thought. Honestly, I didn't know that everyone didn't see and experience the world the way I did. For the first time in my life, I was learning that I had a very distinct perception of life and of others that was most likely the source of my tumultuous past. The good news was that I could finally let myself off the hook for not having the "correct" personality.

While most autistic brains tend to be highly visual, thinking in pictures and visual images, my brain doesn't work that way. Temple Grandin has outlined what she believes are the three

---

[34] Temple Grandin, *The Way I See It*.

different types of autistic minds existing on the spectrum. "By questioning many people, both on and off the spectrum, I have learned that there are three different types of specialized thinking with crossover among these specialized thinking patterns. Determining thinking types in three-year-old children is often not possible. Dominant thinking styles usually become more obvious when a child is seven to nine." [34] Dr. Grandin goes on to describe what she believes to be the three major categories of thinking patterns for those on the autism spectrum.

- Visual thinking/thinking in photorealistic pictures

- Music and math thinking in patterns

- Verbal thinking (not a visual thinker)[35]

I have discovered that I am a verbal and pattern thinker. I don't think in pictures or images like some people on the spectrum; my world is ordered by words. My perception of the world around me is organized in a system of verbal and written communication. The way I navigate the world is by listening and reading. I have no significant ability to visualize anything in my mind, and it is almost as though if it is not written or clearly verbally explained, it doesn't exist for me. I simply cannot comprehend images.

Now this doesn't mean I am unable to see images. Other than the fact that I must wear corrective lenses, I can see fine. I have no physical impairment as it relates to my eyesight. What I have learned is that in my mind's eye, I am usually not able to translate visual images into discernable communication. You know that saying that a picture is worth a thousand words? Well, not so much in my world. This is probably the largest deficit I have to work against in my day-to-day life. This is where my greatest weakness is

---

[35] Temple Grandin, *The Way I See It*.

exposed, and while many people may not understand this aspect of my life, this weakness can be quite debilitating for me.

In 1983, a cultural revolution hit in the world of fashion accessories, and like most kids my age, I wanted in on the newest craze. If you were a child of the eighties like me, then you probably remember the arrival of Swatches. Swatches burst onto the scene and became an official symbol for cool. Every kid wanted one, and every kid would do anything to get one. Swatches gained popularity because they combined the sophistication of Swiss watchmaking with hip and modern eighties fashion design. Swatches were colorful, cool, and made of lightweight plastic. They were excellent accessories for the very colorful decade of the eighties. Among all the things that made Swatches cool, the most significant attraction of the watch was that the face created a new way to tell time. The face of the watch had no numbers.

I could never understand why that bothered me so much. When I was younger, I wanted a Swatch just like every other kid, but when I discovered the watch had no numbers, it made me a little nervous. I wasn't quite able to understand my hesitancy, but looking back, I now understand my objection to perhaps one of the coolest items on the market at the time. My problem was I couldn't "read" the watch because it had no numbers. Using the watch was completely dependent on the owner's ability to visualize the numbers and their placement and to correctly tell the time by using visual imagery rather than written numbers. Simply put, images don't easily translate to information for me, and as a result, I am often left confused and unable to successfully navigate those moments.

Right now, you may be asking why I would associate this small example with being one of my greatest weaknesses. After all, I could just not buy a Swatch, and I should be fine. Certainly, I was not the only child who had a little trouble learning to tell time. Actually, you would be correct, except that the world we live in is extremely visual, probably more than you have noticed, and if you are on the autism spectrum and struggle with visual images like I do, it becomes a very big issue.

Communication is extremely visual. While I'm not certain if there is an accurate percentage of communication that is nonverbal, we must at least acknowledge that communication includes much more than merely the structure of words. Nonverbal communication is an essential part of being able to socially interact with others and navigate the world around you. Without a second thought, most people can instinctively discern the meaning of visual imagery presented in the course of a simple conversation. Facial expressions, body language, and even sitting and standing positions all communicate visual images that need to be deciphered and applied to the context of the verbal communication for the complete interaction to be understood properly.

In the same way I was unable to "read" the watch because it had no written numbers, I am, more often than not, unable to "read" people and conversations because facial expressions, posture, and body language are all visual images instinctively used by others to communicate messages. For the most part, I don't see them because I am not visual. Most people on the autism spectrum would tell you they experience the same thing, but in my case, it is somewhat heightened because I am not a visual thinker but rather a verbal thinker. If you don't literally say it with your words, I will not understand.

This makes relationships complicated. It also makes pastoring a large church extremely complicated. Churches are social gatherings, filled with people who are normally there to engage socially with a community of people who share their belief system. Churches come with a very high set of social expectations, and while I will return to this issue later, I will say now that when it comes to navigating the social construct of the local church, I have some challenges that I am willing to face head on, but that I also understand will always be challenging for me.

The phenomenon of being unable to see visual expressions of communication in social settings is often referred to as "mind blindness." Once I was exposed to this concept, it made it easier for me to understand how I process the world around me. Having a good grasp of my inability to consistently process visual images into communication helped me to understand a few of the reasons why I am completely disturbed by lack of clear verbal communication. When words are not clear, neither am I, and the result often leaves me in distress.

When your world is structured primarily by words, it creates a world that is neatly ordered and defined. In my world, the power to define is the power to direct. Words create order, structure, and symmetry. Words create identity and intention. Words provide stability and security. If it can be described and defined, then I am fine. This creates an extremely rigid system of thinking which, in turn, leads to an extremely linear lifestyle.

As well as being extremely literal, people on the autism spectrum often follow rigid routines. I do both, and I would venture to say I am more likely to rate higher on the scale because I am not a visual thinker like most autistic minds. Visual thinkers have some room to interpret what they see. Images and symbolism provide a bit more flexibility because visual thinkers can interpret those images. Words are definite and usually have a more static meaning. Words mean what they mean and leave very little room for interpretation. When you are a verbal thinker like me, life is extremely black and white.

Many of my struggles are a result of my rigid and sometimes narrow perspective of the world. Life on the spectrum often means life inside the lines—lines that are well-defined. Those lines also include how my brain forces my senses to process incoming information. Most people on the autism spectrum struggle with sensory issues, and until I was diagnosed, I just assumed everyone processed their environment the same way I did. My senses operate along very strict lines, which means every bit of information my five senses encounter is very pronounced and distinct.

When I enter an environment, my senses don't often blend together to help my brain process the environment collectively. What I experience are distinct sounds, smells, and at times textures that create the environment. It is not uncommon for me to be able to hear each sound that constitutes the aggregate noise in a room. While most people hear noise, I can hear every note and pitch that makes up that noise. The term for this is sensory overload or sensory processing disorder.

Normally, if I am to survive any crowded and noisy setting, I have to have a focal point, a sound that attracts my sense of sound by distracting it from searching for all of the other sounds in a room. It is not uncommon for me to accomplish that by using a set of wireless headphones that accompany me most places I go. Music normally works because it is organized noise where the sounds involved all have a unified direction and stay clearly within the limits of their lines as defined by the musical arrangement.

Living on the autism spectrum also means that I am weak at recognizing facial expressions. Ironically, this issue doesn't just affect my ability to read other people's faces; it also affects people's ability to read my facial expressions. People with autism/Asperger's often have what is known as a flat affect. This simply means that their facial expressions don't mirror the emotions of the environment or social context. This can be problematic because it sometimes looks as though I am completely disengaged and disinterested in what is taking place all around me, and that is often far from the truth. One of the most consistent criticisms I receive is that I need to smile more. I'm told quite often that I look mean and far too serious.

Almost every time I receive those remarks, I am perplexed as to why people feel that way. I can be completely oblivious to how I look to others. Honestly, this issue has been a source of great frustration for me. Many times, the setting is one that suggests my facial expressions should communicate excitement and joy, but most often the only emotion they can associate with my expressions are anger, frustration, and fatigue. Now, there are times when I may actually be feeling those emotions, but more often than not, I get a bad reputation for something I am not always aware of or am unable to control. In fact, it was one of the primary grievances brought against me during my candidacy for the role of lead pastor in the church in which I now serve.

Equally difficult for me is the task of reading facial expressions. My autistic mind is not always able to identify and translate facial expressions into defined forms of communication. Prior to receiving an official diagnosis, I took an online assessment aimed at helping me discover my ability to read facial expressions. Let me first say that, until this assessment, I had no earthly idea that so many facial expressions even existed. In my very well-defined, black-and-white, word-ordered world, only a few facial expressions existed. Happy, sad, angry, and perhaps confused, but even that one is a little too ambiguous for me to read well. In essence, anyone who communicates to me in anything other than words will have a hard time getting me to completely understand them.

Getting an official diagnosis of autism spectrum disorder was in many ways like being reborn. Most of my life had now become obsolete, or it at least felt that way. Having lived thirty-six years in a continual state of "mind blindness" caused me to rethink most of my significant life events and relationships. Much of my life began to come into focus, and I began to see myself in an entirely new way. What I thought I knew about life, relationships, and myself was changing fast. The most significant of all the revelations about life was the fact that everything I thought I knew about God was going to change in a way that would dramatically change the course of my life forever.

## God and Disabilities

One day at a small private Christian school, the teachers and faculty decided to plan a schoolwide picnic. After weeks of planning, the teachers and students gathered together in the school's courtyard to enjoy some time together eating their favorite foods and playing their favorite games.

The tables were set up nicely, and all of the food was placed on the table, ready for the teachers and students to enjoy together. One teacher, realizing she had a few selfish boys in her class, placed a sign on one end of the table next to a bowl of apples. The sign read, "Take only one apple each. God is watching." One young boy walked down to the end of the table, read the sign, and went running down to the other end of the table with a sheet of paper in one hand and a marker in the other. After about five minutes, the boy placed his paper next to a gigantic plate full of chocolate chip cookies. Noticing what the young boy had just done, his teacher walked down to the far end of the table to see what the note said. To her surprise, the young boy had written his own sign instructing his fellow classmates on how to behave. His sign read, "Take all the cookies you want. God is watching the apples."

When it comes to God and disabilities, we may sometimes feel as though God was so busy watching someone or something else that He dropped the ball on making sure that everyone else turned out okay. I cannot claim to have full understanding of what someone with a physical limitation may have to endure on a daily basis, and because of that lack of experience, I am careful to attach such a label to myself. Autism spectrum disorder is often characterized as a developmental disability because it is not, nor should it be, classified as a mental illness.

Despite my limited experience with being physically disabled, I do now have a special new concept of my own struggles in life in the context of lacking the ability to do certain things that others can do. For me, some of the things I can't do leave me with some glaring weaknesses. No matter what limitations a person faces, one thing we all instinctively know is that there is a tremendous impact on a person's faith and spirituality when it comes to living with a disability or a limitation.

As a Christian and a pastor, I developed a deep desire to understand how my diagnosis would affect me spiritually. I wanted and needed to explore the role of God, faith, and the Bible in my new understanding of myself, my exposure to my limitations, and in some ways what felt like my brokenness.

> In 1 Corinthians 12:14-27, the apostle Paul describes the church using the metaphor of the human body. He said that "God arranged the members in the body, each one of them, as he chose" (v. 18). Some parts he describes as weaker but indispensable and others as less honorable and less respectable but treated with special honor and greater respect (vv.22-23). Certainly on one level Paul is describing people with disabilities, broken people, as a part of Christ's body, the new community. And his description of the Christian community should be understood as normative, as what we should see when we walk into church.[36]

According to Paul, God is not just watching the apples, God is also keeping an eye on the cookies. The community of faith includes those who are limited and broken in various ways, and the point of the inclusion is not just to make them whole, but to make the community whole by including them as part of the body. Perhaps the issue I'm facing is not just about my ability to understand the role of faith in the discovery of my limits, but also about how to appropriate Paul's words into a vision of community for the physically and mentally limited. "The problem is that Christian people generally have an inadequate understanding of God's role in disabilities."[37]

If you're feeling a little overwhelmed by that statement, it's okay. I am overwhelmed, too. Truth is, faith has always had a rather ambiguously strained relationship with disabilities and limitations. It can be difficult to believe in a perfect creator who would either create or allow some members of the body to be born

---

[36]Michael S. Bates, *Disability & The Gospel*.

[37]Michael S. Bates, *Disability & The Gospel*.

or to develop a weakness. How does God create an autistic boy and then, decades later, compel him to follow a conviction that he must become a pastor?

Moses is perhaps one of the most interesting figures in the Bible and is still to this day an icon not only in Christianity but in pop culture as well. Moses has become symbolic with freedom because of his incredible story. Moses is larger-than-life, yet many times we forget the profound limitations that he had, limitations he believed should have disqualified him from being considered for service to God.

> But Moses pleaded with the Lord, "O Lord I'm not very good with words. I never have been, and I'm not now, even though you have spoken to me. I get tongue-tied, and my words get tangled." Then the Lord asked Moses, "Who makes a person's mouth? Who decides whether people speak or do not speak, hear or do not hear, see or do not see? Is it not I, the Lord?"[38]

This is perhaps one of the most unsettling yet sobering statements in the Bible. It totally changed my perception of God and of myself, and I'm hoping that when it comes to God and disabilities, it will change your perception, too.

> In this startling response, God not only does not deny responsibility for conditions we normally consider disabilities (blindness, deafness, muteness); rather to our surprise, God takes credit for them! God says these things come from and are made by him. This is a hard statement! And we must accept it and learn from it. [39]

---

[38]Exodus 4:10-11 NLT.

[39]Michael S. Bates, *Disability & The Gospel.*

The idea that God would take credit for the disability that Moses has is eye-opening, to say the least. According to God, there is a process by which a decision is made in determining a person's abilities. What's interesting about this perception is that it calls us to critique our understanding of disabilities. God seems to suggest that the types of abilities a person possesses are the result of strategy, planning, and purpose. His conversation with Moses in no way suggests that speaking or not speaking differentiates a person in the eyes of God. In fact, the lack of the ability to speak is not presented by God as a defect at all. It is merely presented as a part of God's creative abilities. "We must revisit our deeply ensconced cultural assumptions about what it means to be 'normal' as opposed to what it might mean to live for years in a state that must be considered 'brokenness.'" [40]

When it comes to God's role in the lives of those we consider disabled or differently abled, God seems to take a much different approach to how they should be viewed. What appears to be a glaring weakness and an obstacle that stands in the way of living a full life may very well be an opportunity. God's involvement with the weak and disabled points to an opportunity to recognize God in the face of the frailty of our human bodies. One of the greatest examples of how to change our view of disabilities from a weakness to a strength is found in Paul's admission of his mysterious "thorn."

## Theology of "Thorns"

History has a way of robbing us of our humanity. The stories we often tell others and ourselves about us don't always match our true stories. We almost always succumb to the temptation to retell our tales with exaggeration instead of exactness. It is human nature. It is who we are, and if we are to be completely honest, we prefer to sanitize every part of our human experience in an effort to not only exalt ourselves but also explain away our faults and failures. This is a great mistake. The flaws and failures of our human experience,

---

[40]Michael S. Bates, *Disability & The Gospel*.

though not considered good, are in fact more than good. They are gifts from God.

Until my diagnosis, the majority of my life was spent redacting my own story in order to explain away the parts of my life that made me and others uncomfortable. Similarly, there are parts of my story that I conveniently omit because the culture we live in demands that we edit out all of our flaws. We are the social media generation, the generation that creates a following by creating, managing, and editing our profiles in an attempt to produce popularity. We don't want to be flawed. We resist being human, and anything that remotely reminds us of our humanity is removed from our narrative.

A kindergarten teacher was walking around her class, checking in on her students to see how they were progressing on their art assignment. Pleased with what she was seeing, she continued to move about the room, slowly passing by each child's desk and periodically pausing and offering words of praise and affirmation to her young pupils. She rounded the corner toward the back of her classroom, and as she approached young Sarah, she saw what looked to be the beginning stages of an interesting art project. The teacher leaned over to get a closer look at Sarah's picture. When she was unable to discern what the picture was, she said to her, "Sarah, that's an interesting picture, what are you drawing?" Without looking up, Sarah replied, "I'm drawing a picture of God!" Stunned for a brief moment, the teacher chuckled and said to Sarah, "Oh honey, no one really knows what God looks like." Without so much of a flinch of confusion, Sarah confidently replied, "They will when I'm done with my picture!"

The moral of that story is that perhaps the best picture of who God actually is can come from the most unlikely of sources. Perhaps in our haste to rid ourselves of our humanity, we have in fact distorted the best pictures of God that we could ever see. I know this reality all too well because I have practiced redacting my story for so long that the picture that God was painting in my life became distorted. The way I viewed myself and the way we view weakness is more often than not a distorted picture of God.

If you grew up in the Christian faith, then chances are you probably heard of a guy named Paul. Even if you didn't grow up in or around the Christian church and are not familiar with the Bible, you have probably heard from Paul. Paul is the guy who told us that the love of money is the source of all kinds of evil. If you've ever been to a wedding, you've probably heard from Paul who tells us how love is patient, kind, and never gives up. Paul is also the guy who coined one the most popular phrases used when dealing with a person or issue that has become a constant source of aggravation. It was Paul who gave us the phrase "a thorn in my flesh."

Although we most often use this phrase to describe something or someone who is annoying, Paul's use of the phrase was linked to a much more serious issue he was facing. In a rare moment of self-disclosure, Paul exposes his audience to the reality that he suffered from something that he begged God to remove, only to have God deny his request every single time.

We know a lot about Paul now, but we have some distinct advantages that his original audience didn't. We can read all of Paul's work to all the churches to which he was communicating. His collection of letters that make up a large part of what we know as the New Testament weren't really part of a collection at the time he wrote them. We can learn a lot about Paul by the way he wrote, the things he shared, and beliefs he held. We can put together the pieces of his work like a puzzle and construct our view of Paul, one that is not always completely accurate.

First-century Christians certainly knew Paul—some of them may have even known him as Saul—but we don't gain any real insight into Paul's personal pains and problems in life until he invites us into his life in his second letter to the Corinthian church. Paul sort of eases us into a moment of transparency and truth about his life and ministry. As he moves through his letter, we get a sense that Paul shares in the commonality of human struggle when it comes to self-worth and self-awareness.

While we herald Paul as one of the greatest of all time—and he was one of the greats—he was a great writer and probably not all that great of a public speaker. In fact, Paul himself admits to this weakness, saying, "I may be unskilled as a speaker, but I am not lacking in knowledge."[41] It's at this point in his letter when we begin to see Paul shift from superhuman status to being human just like the rest of us. I believe this moment of authenticity sets the stage for what is, in my opinion, the most transparent text in the entire Bible.

By the end of chapter 11, Paul is baring it all. He exposes us to all of the tragic and trying times that he faces as a leader in the Christian movement. We get to experience a Paul who has experienced some very painful moments that perhaps we had overlooked prior to this point. In his effort to humanize himself and his personal and private struggles with life and faith, Paul shares that he has often gone hungry and thirsty. He has been physically beaten and gone extended periods of time without sleep. He wants us to know his moments of weakness when he says, "If I must boast, I would rather boast about the things that show how weak I am."[42] What we will learn about Paul in the next chapter is that although we consider him to be strong because of all that he has accomplished, Paul considers himself to be weak, and it's his weakness that God uses to produce strength.

> ...to keep me from becoming proud, I was given a thorn in my flesh, a messenger from Satan to torment me and keep me from becoming proud. Three different times I begged the Lord to take it away. Each time he said, "My grace is all you need. My power works best in weakness." So now I am glad to

---

[41]2 Corinthians 11:6 NLT.

[42]2 Corinthians 11:30 NLT.

boast about my weaknesses, so that the power of Christ can work through me. That's why I take pleasure in my weaknesses, and in the insults, hardships, persecutions, and troubles that I suffer for Christ. For when I am weak, then I am strong. [43]

Above all the painful experiences in Paul's life, there was only one issue that he literally begged God to get rid of. Paul's life wasn't easy by any stretch of the imagination, so for all intents and purposes, we can assume that Paul was not a wimp. What I find both interesting and inspiring about Paul is that the thing he struggled with the most was the thing that was most unseen about his life.

Scholars have engaged in heated debates as to just what Paul's "thorn" could have been. There's a whole school of thought that contends that his "thorn" was an actual person or a group of people. Some even suggest it had something to do with the groups of people who ridiculed Paul for not being an eloquent speaker. It's an interesting theory, to say the least. Then there are other schools of thought that say Paul's "thorn" was some sort of physical limitation of disability Paul had. Speculation in this area ranges from poor eyesight to epilepsy and reoccurring seizures. The truth is Paul never really says exactly what the issue is. What we do know is that it is something that Paul doesn't want to deal with at all.

Pleading with God three times is much more than a casual and occasional request for some sort of divine relief. What seems like periodic prayers are actually prolonged sessions of praying and begging. When Paul shares that he pleaded with God, what he is communicating is the sense of urgency and passion in praying that God not just relieve him of the pain caused by this issue but remove the issue altogether because of its tremendous impact on his quality of life. We may never be totally sure what Paul's "thorn" was, and

---

[43]2 Corinthians 12:7-10 NLT.

maybe that's for the best because it makes room for each of us to identify our own "thorns."

I have been a Christian for a long time, and I have been reading the Bible for a very long time. Until I was diagnosed with autism spectrum disorder, I was never more moved by any portion of the Bible, including this story even though I must have read it hundreds of times. I can vividly remember turning to these verses the week following my diagnosis, with the overwhelming flood of emotions that came with finally having a definition for my differences. After reading them, I wept. I always knew I was weak, but I had finally discovered just how strong God really was.

# CHAPTER 7
# I AM HUMAN

## Learning to Listen

Over the years, I've been described in a lot of interesting and inflammatory ways. What I know now is that some of my characteristics came from my being on the autism spectrum, and those characteristics earned me some pretty interesting nicknames. Of all the names that I have been called over the years, the one that always stuck out to me was "robot." I suppose I earned that nickname because I tend to be very stoic. As a kid, being so made me a target because it made other kids want to provoke me into a visible emotional response. As an adult, I earned the "robot" moniker because I very seldom demonstrated any emotions at all. I guess you can't please everyone, even when they are trying to find a label to define you.

Autism is a spectrum, which makes it extremely difficult to understand. No two people on the autism spectrum are alike, and no one set of issues and challenges is the same for all people on the spectrum. Autism is almost an invisible illness. It can't really be seen, and for people like me who seem to function well, it may be almost impossible to detect because any behaviors associated with it may be seen only as character flaws or indifference.

When I was diagnosed, I immediately entered into an already heated debate about autism and labels. Should we use the term "high-functioning" when referring to people like me on the spectrum who are able to verbalize their struggles? What about the millions of parents whose children are nonverbal? Is it appropriate to create a label for them that suggests they are somehow deficient because they are not "high-functioning" and need more support and services? How do we determine the degree to which people on the spectrum are impacted by their autism?

If I am to be completely honest, I am not sure how to make sense of the many facets of this ongoing debate. People have passionately given their lives and their money to promote their perspective on autism and in most cases rightfully so. Autism is complicated. Autism truly is a spectrum, and because of that, it is almost impossible to come up with a consistent opinion from those who are most closely affected by it.

While I'm not willing to stand on my ability to accurately understand the science of autism, I am intrigued by the significance of my own encounter with autism spectrum disorder. Stepping into this world has caused me to develop a much greater appreciation for my own humanity and the humanity of those around me. In a world that has crowded out the need to fully appreciate the heart of humanity, I am captured by the discovery of my own lifelong struggle in a way that compels me to communicate how sacred life is. Life is sacred not because we are different. Life is sacred because when it comes down to it, we are all the same; we are all human.

Today my wife and I have three beautiful boys, but I can vividly recall the discussion about having another baby. At the time, we had two boys, and my boys loved their mother to death. I was cool. I was fun to hang out with occasionally. I was even needed for special tasks, but when it came to who had their little hearts, it was obvious that their hearts belonged to their mother.

I knew I needed to act swiftly. My plan was to convince my wife to try for a little girl. My pitch to her was that I just wanted someone to celebrate me when I came home from a long day of work like my boys celebrated her. Hey, I'm human; I wanted to feel the love, too, and I just knew that having a little girl would solve my problem. Well, I've already told you that we have three boys, so you know how my plan turned out. Here's what I learned as a result—three children are a *huge* responsibility.

What's amazing about this story is that our oldest son tried to warn us. When my wife and I sat our two boys down to tell them that they may have a little brother or sister, our oldest son, who was around seven at the time, sat back in his chair, rubbed his hand on his little chin, and said "Three kids…that's a lot of kids to take care of." Turns out he was right! Our house is constantly a mess; in fact, it is a mess right now. My wife and I clean nonstop because the truth is we live with three messy little people.

Messiness in our home has a large scope of impact. Living with three messy little people is always interesting, constantly tiring, and sometimes frustrating, yet we have learned how to live together, laugh together, and love each other despite the fact that life gets a little messy. When I was diagnosed with autism spectrum disorder, it was a lot like the day we announced to our sons we were having another child. All I could think about was how much work it was going to be. I knew it was going to get a little messy. I could either fold those unfolded clothes and put them away or just close the door and pretend I didn't see them. I knew I was finally going to be forced to face my own issues, my own struggles, and my own humanity.

I've always loved music. Music is a huge part of my life. Next to reading, it has probably been one of the primary tools that helped me cope with my lack of social skills over the years. I once heard a story that illustrates both the power of music and the power of a listening ear.

One day, a group of musicians wanted to test the cliché that music can calm the savage beast. Enlisting one of the world's most accomplished violinists, the group decided to test the theory by taking her out to the Serengeti, a place populated with lions. Once they had made their way into the most densely populated area, they dropped the expert violinist off, connected her sound system, and told her to begin playing.

Within minutes, animals of all kinds were making their way toward the music. One by one, they slowly approached the speakers, and almost as if in a trance, they sat quietly at her feet, obviously soothed by the beautiful music that was being played. Then all of a sudden, an enormous lion sprang out of the brush and approached the violinist at top speed. Standing just inches away from her, he reared back on his hind legs, and with one swipe of his gigantic paw, he struck the violinist across the face, knocking her to the ground.

The lion next to him became irate. He turned to him and growled, "What are you doing? Didn't you hear the beautiful music she was playing?" The second lion leaned back with a puzzled look on his face, cupped a paw around his right ear, and replied, "I'm sorry, what did you say?"

Learning that I was autistic meant taking the time to listen long enough to enjoy the beautiful music that was playing as the soundtrack of my life. Like many people, I found myself guilty of ignoring what was beautiful about my life, simply because I either could not or would not listen. A large part of me had settled into my label. Perhaps I was a "robot" or maybe something other than human. It's not surprising how many of us find ourselves subconsciously living up to the labels society has stuck us with and how often it subtly impairs our ability to listen well. Like many people, I had adjusted to the label I was given, and as a result, I lacked the will to listen to the possibility that I may be something more than everyone believed about me.

Listening takes courage. It is much easier to go around taking swipes at anyone or anything that you consider to be a noisemaker, but the reality is that some of what we think is noise may actually be what nudges us closer to embracing our humanity. Listening was what finally gave me the courage to embrace my own. Listening to others was a big challenge. It was one of the hardest things I have ever had to do. Still, as difficult as it was to finally learn how to listen to the people around me, the biggest challenge of adjusting to my new diagnosis was learning to listen to my limits.

## Listening to My Limits

No one likes limits. We all see limits as a threat. Limits seem to pose a threat to our ability to achieve complete autonomy. We don't want anything or anyone to control us or influence our choices. Everyone struggles with limits and boundaries. Perhaps that's why embracing our human limitations is inherently difficult; we don't like being told what we cannot do. We love to live on the edge of what is possible. We all love to push ourselves to the max and then push ourselves just a little further. We do this with our time, our money, and our emotions. We push way beyond our spiritual, mental, and emotional budgets, oftentimes writing proverbial checks that we lack the funds to cover.

When I was younger, I suffered from a variety of odd medical mysteries. It was not uncommon for me to periodically go to the doctor to be tested for some strange medical issue I was having. Many of the issues I had would eventually subside, leaving us with no answer as to the cause. There was, however, one recurring issue that never seemed to resolve itself. No matter what we tried, I continued to have migraine headaches.

I still occasionally have migraines, and I have learned something about what I believe to be the source of my headaches. It has helped me manage them far greater than any medicine that I have been prescribed in the past. I have learned that a large part of my migraine problem was the result of allowing myself to wander outside of my limitations, limits that I had no idea existed until I was diagnosed with autism spectrum disorder.

In 2010, when my family moved to Lagrange, I found myself at the apex of my migraine problems. Only a few weeks into coming on staff at New Community Church, I begin to feel a resurgence of these debilitating headaches in ways I had not experienced in quite a while. Prior to my arrival in Lagrange, I had worked with my doctor to find medication that would help me. It was working well, and I was even noticing that I had them less frequently. As always, there was no physical reason noted that could serve as a source for my problem, so my doctor made sure I found ways to manage my stress levels.

I should have known it then, but for some reason, I didn't connect the dots until much later. I knew that stress had everything to do with my migraine problem I just didn't know exactly what was stressing me out all the time. Learning the why and the how as it relates to our human limitations can save us a lot of time, money, and residual stress. When it came to treating my headache problem, I focused on getting rid of the headaches without totally understanding that the headaches marked the boundary to my human limits.

God understands limits far better than we do. In fact, God encourages us to observe limits not as means of restricting our progress, but as the primary tool for protecting it. One of the best examples of this principle is found in the story of the Ten Commandments.

To understand and appreciate this story for its greater significance, we should take a look at the context of the commandments. When we catch up to Moses and the people of Israel in Exodus chapter 20, we peek in on a broken group of people who have spent literally hundreds of years in captivity and have now been rescued by their God. Not only did God rescue them from Egypt, but He also had big plans to give them their own land.

The long-awaited day of departure had come for Israel, and as they moved with anticipation toward their next stage of life as a people, God had them pause in the middle of their progress so that he could teach them a very valuable principle about pride and boundaries. Exactly two months after leaving Egypt, God led them into the wilderness of Sinai. After speaking with Moses privately, God instructed Moses to "Mark off a boundary all around the mountain. Warn the people, 'Be careful! Do not go up on the mountain or even touch its boundaries. Anyone who touches the mountain will certainly be put to death.'" [44] After years of living in captivity, God was giving the people of Israel the freedom for

---

[44]Exodus 19:12 NLT.

which they had prayed for centuries, and in a strange way, God seemed to set the stage for freedom by establishing clear boundaries, boundaries that they dare not cross unless they wanted to taste death.

In many ways, I think the key to real freedom is to recognize one's limits. In Exodus chapter 20, God gives Moses a set of core values for his people to live by. These "commandments" could really be God's way of giving humanity some guiding principles to help them maintain and manage their freedom. What's significant about this list is that God actually gives a command to observe the limits of humanity by implementing an idea called Sabbath. "Remember to observe the Sabbath day by keeping it holy. You have six days each week for your ordinary work, but the seventh day is a Sabbath day of rest dedicated to the Lord your God."[45] While there can be ongoing debate about the practice of Sabbath, the meaning is much more about practicing a discipline than observing a particular day of the week. Sabbath was all about limits and how to embrace them in order to truly live a healthy spiritual, mental, and emotional life.

Life without limits sounds exciting, but limits are a gift. Limits are a guide that points us to our greatest potential. Without limits, we become overloaded. To protect our potential, we need spiritual, mental, and emotional margins. "Emotional overload saps our strength, paralyzes our resolve, and maximizes our vulnerability, leaving the door open for even further margin erosion."[46] Learning to be strong ultimately means learning to live within our human limitations. When Paul exposes us to his ongoing struggle with his "thorn," he points us to a truth we often ignore—we are at our strongest when we identify where our weaknesses begin.

We all struggle with this in ways so profound that we have yet to discover the depths to which this idea affects us. In many ways,

---

[45]Exodus 20:8-9 NLT.

[46]Richard Swenson, *Margin*.

we have created a new sense of what it means to be human without realizing that our quest for unlimited resources, unlimited access, and unlimited strength has created an unrealistic expectation of what it means to be human. We have dehumanized ourselves, giving ourselves a false sense of importance and yet at the same time making ourselves nothing special at all. The world we live in now has unfortunately made it easy for people to ignore their own pain and suffering. The world we have created continues to make it easier for people to ignore limits, limits that often save us from hurting ourselves beyond healing.

Hopelessness is the product of the gradual dehumanization of humanity. When we ignore the limits of our own human capacity, we lack the ability look beyond ourselves for the strength, love, and security found in a relationship with God and a relationship with one another. When Paul comes to grips with his "thorn," he makes an assumption that the purpose of the thorn is not to give him pain but to keep him from becoming proud. What if our limits are a gift from God that keeps us mindful of our inability to be totally self-sufficient? What if our proverbial thorns are designed to do exactly what Paul suggests his did, prevent us from the trap of pride that eats away at our humanity?

For years, I lived an unrealistic life that pushed me well beyond my human limitations, and it resulted in my slowly becoming more and more disconnected from the real me. The most troubling part of living this way is that I had spent so much time chipping away at my own humanity that I began to struggle to see the humanity in others. If I was going to attempt to be something more than human, I expected others to attempt it, too. If I was going to ignore my limits, I fully expected others to push themselves beyond what is human.

The problems we face in our current culture can often be rooted in this very issue. This one is bigger than just me wrestling with characteristics associated with autism, this is about the human insistence on becoming bigger than our boundaries. When we *forget* that we are human, we forget that we are *human.* When we dismiss our own humanity, we create a breeding ground for all sorts of heinous acts against humanity. We teach ourselves and our children not to feel. We teach ourselves and our children to do away with our basic human instinct to have compassion and empathy for the weak and oppressed. We teach ourselves and our children to ignore our duty to the world around us. The absence of boundaries breeds a culture that lacks humility, and a lack of humility always results in a lack of humanity.

In a strange way, learning that I was autistic helped restore my sense of humanity and at the same time helped restore my faith in humanity. Learning that I was autistic helped me focus more on finding out where my boundaries were. I was no longer interested in pushing through and putting off the importance of managing my life in ways that produced the most health for me, for the first time in my life, I began to see boundaries as a blessing. When I was diagnosed with autism spectrum disorder, I discovered three major boundaries that I had been unknowingly compromising, and when I made some simple adjustments, I begin to see substantial improvement in my life and relationships.

## Emotional Boundaries

Life as a pastor can be an emotional roller coaster. Every day promises twists, turns, and flips that all come fast and forceful. There is almost never a day where I don't receive some news, report, or rumor that doesn't directly impact my emotional state of mind. Living life as a husband and father also adds to my daily dose of roller coaster activity, and this is all without taking into consideration that living on the autism spectrum can be a task all by itself.

Establishing healthy emotional boundaries first means understanding when your emotional boundaries are challenged. One of the most significant sources of strain on my emotional boundaries is social anxiety. Life on the autism spectrum often means dealing with a sometimes intense fear of navigating social settings. It's not uncommon for me to retreat into my "cave" when feeling overwhelmed with too much social activity. As a pastor, this can be extremely challenging because most of my responsibility requires me to socialize with people, sometimes people I don't personally know very well. Don't get me wrong, I love to be around people, but being on the autism spectrum means that doing so takes an enormous amount of emotional energy. Socializing is like a sprint. I can do it, but not for long periods of time. Even though I have a desire to meet the social needs of others, I have had to learn the hard way how to listen to my limits and retreat.

Jesus faced some similar challenges, and although I'm not claiming him to have been on the autism spectrum, I think we can all learn how to listen to our limits and create healthy emotional boundaries for ourselves.

> "Jesus went out to the lake with his disciples, and a large crowd followed him. They came from all over Galilee, Judea, Jerusalem, Idumea, from east of the Jordan River, and even from as far north as Tyre and Sidon. The news about his miracles had spread far and wide, and vast numbers of people came to see him. Jesus instructed his disciples to have a boat ready so the crowd would not crush him."[47]

Crowds crush me. I don't attend large concerts because crowds crush me. I go to the movies in the middle of the day when there are fewer people there because crowds crush me. I try desperately to avoid going to huge conferences and workshops because crowds crush me. It took me a long while to figure this out, but being diagnosed on the autism spectrum helped to clarify this critical boundary. I had never been able to address it before. Prior to my diagnosis, I had always just been considered shy or antisocial, labels that often do more damage than good to a person. I had spent most of my life trying to fit in with the crowd, and the harsh

---

[47]Mark 3:7-9 NLT.

reality was that I would never be one of the "crowd" because it was my attempts to be a part of the crowd that were crushing my spirit.

When it comes to emotional boundaries, what is it that crushes you? As an autistic pastor, a person whose job it was to socialize with crowds of people, this revelation came at a hefty price, but it allowed me to finally grab hold of my own humanity in ways that would help me organize my life and in ways that assisted me in my task of pastoring instead of assassinating me in the process.

I am unable to avoid the responsibility of socializing with my congregation, but I was able to adopt a few practices that have proven to be beneficial in helping me maintain my emotional margin. First off, I began to work from home on Tuesdays. I have many pastor friends and colleagues, and most that I know take off Mondays. I completely understand this need because, quite honestly, Sundays can be quite draining, even if you're not autistic. Every person needs to find ways to build healthy emotional boundaries, and one of those ways is to schedule it. Believe it or not, most people exceed their emotional limits simply because they have no scheduled alone time. When I was diagnosed with autism, this became extremely important for me because I most naturally wanted and needed a significant amount of alone time. Socializing on Sundays in addition to preaching weekly in front of a crowd can and will drain me emotionally, spiritually, and physically.

When I began to notice a pattern of emotional instability, I quickly recognized that I was exceeding my human capacity for social interaction, and I was suffering the consequences weekly. Migraines, mood swings, and mental anguish were a weekly reality until I learned to build boundaries. Tuesdays are perfect for me because that's usually the day when I am most exhausted emotionally. I like to meet with my staff on Mondays so that we can set the course for the week, and then I use Tuesdays to regroup. After only a few weeks of implementing this new system, I discovered that I am much more productive and pleasant when I have my regularly scheduled time to retreat into myself without interruption.

Second, I try very hard to have control over my social interactions. When you lead a church, especially a midsized church like mine, people expect to be able to socialize with you to some degree. I confess that until I was diagnosed with autism, I was virtually clueless to this need. It was not uncommon for me to speak Sunday morning and then disappear backstage for a few minutes after my closing prayer, giving me just enough time to scout out the room and find the quickest route to my office without having to actually speak to anyone. Delivering a message is already a spiritual draining experience, but for me, it can cause anxiety attacks if I'm not fully prepared. This often requires my mind to be in a very healthy place, and in the past, it almost always required solitude immediately preceding the weekend services.

The problem I began to encounter was that my failure to interact socially with my congregation was subtly undermining my ability to lead effectively. I had to make a critical decision as to how I could fulfill my duties as a pastor and maintain some healthy emotional boundaries. Most pastors use the time following the service to interact with their members, but I knew that would not be possible for me. Instead, I began to greet people as they were being seated in our auditorium before the service started. Now this did require an adjustment on my part. It meant I had to be prepared to deliver the message and be able to interact with people prior to preaching. The adjustment I had to make required a greater level of focus during the week. It also required that I be just as prepared to socially interact with people as I was to preach a message to them.

Finally, I learned that to create emotionally healthy boundaries, I would need help in managing my time. People who know me extremely well would tell you that I am a stickler for time management. It's almost as though I have a fascination with time. Time is what dictates and defines my life in a way that brings necessary order and clarity. I abhor being late, and I am equally as anxious about arriving or beginning anything before the allotted time. I would later learn that not everyone shared my love for timeliness. Routine is one of my closest companions. Being autistic can at times make me extremely rigid when it comes to time and time management, and while I am able to adequately manage my time in isolation, being a pastor rarely allows me to fend off constant interruptions and inconveniences.

Having a trusted team of people that can help me manage my daily and weekly distractions has a tremendous impact on how I am able to successfully navigate leading a large church. In order to maintain my health, my team helps me manage everything from phone calls to meetings and social activities. I have a great staff of people who are extremely sensitive to my needs and understand and support my need to retreat as well as my need for routine. For them to help me, I have to be completely transparent about how I am feeling, where I am, and where I need to be. They have access to my complete schedule so that they can ensure I am not exceeding my emotional capacity. They even have access and the authority to schedule my appointments, check my emails, and respond to voice messages on my behalf. All of these basic principles assist me with the next very important way that I embrace my humanity by learning to develop schedule boundaries.

## Time and Schedule Boundaries

Properly managing my time and schedule has a direct effect on my emotional well-being, but being on the autism spectrum presents me with some challenges as related to time and schedule. I am naturally a creature of habit. I need repetition. I often tell my staff that routine, repetition, and habit help me to see clearly, therefore what I do with my time is not always as important as having a playbook for time. As much as possible, I need a set schedule. I have discovered that any deviations from my schedule have the potential for devastating effects on my mental health and my motivation.

I am at my strongest when I have a system. Managing my time and schedule begins with shining a light on my activities to determine which activities offer a reasonable return on my investment. When Paul speaks openly and candidly about his thorn,

111

he reminds us twice that facing the reality of our humanity is what illuminates our path to emotional, mental, and spiritual health and strength. Creating a time and schedule margin becomes extremely important because if I could, I would never stop, never sleep, and never surrender to the moments when I know I should observe some form of Sabbath.

Most people are that way. We live in a culture that doesn't know how to say no to more. We try to cram more activity in a twenty-four-hour period than is humanly possible, and when we accomplish a task of any size, even at the expense of Sabbath, we are actually proud. We live in a culture that brags about how many hours we work each week. Our culture idolizes those who never sleep or call in sick from work. We have dehumanized ourselves by attempting to override our body's natural need for mental and emotional boundaries, and we are proud of it.

You may have also fallen into the trap of ignoring your own humanity in order to produce more than is humanly possible. In many ways, finding out that I was autistic helped me to make peace with my mortality. I had to learn that I was not supposed to be able to accomplish more than was humanly possible. God created a twenty-four-hour day for a reason, and the key to my success was to learn to invest my time and not spend it.

Paul writes about the proper use of time in Ephesians chapter 5 when he encourages the early church to live under the light of Christ, a light that helps us examine how we manage the valuable time that God has gifted us. "So be careful how you live. Don't live like fools, but like those who are wise. Make the most opportunity in these evil days. Don't act thoughtlessly, but understand what the Lord wants you to do."[48]

I often spend the end of most days thinking "this day was evil," and I'm sure you've had those days, too, but that's not exactly what Paul is talking about. When Paul makes the comment that the days

---

[48]Ephesians 5:15-17 NLT.

are full of evil, he is making a reference to the Genesis story in which the penalty for sin resulted in hard labor for humanity. In other words, Paul is saying that every day is going to be hard work. Being an adult with autism is hard work. Everyday life is hard labor even with the little things, so in the words of Paul, I have to "make the most of every opportunity" by using my faith as the filter for determining how to invest my time.

## Increasing the Margin of Error

One of the distinguishing factors of autism is a type of hyper-focus on an area of interest. Most people on the spectrum find that they are drawn to certain hobbies or subjects and as a result become "experts" on that topic. It is not uncommon for a person on the autism spectrum to spend hours of time engaged in their favorite activity. This can also be demonstrated by an intense focus on one activity at a time. It can be difficult for them to focus on other tasks until the task they are engaged in is completed.

Until I was diagnosed with autism, I didn't understand that everyone didn't experience the world this way. I consider myself to be an extremely focused person, particularly when it directly relates to my interests. If allowed, I could spend hours engaged in my own interests, but up until I was diagnosed, I was unable to understand that most people are able to do more than one activity at a time. Instead, what I saw was a lack of commitment and focus, and this mindset left me blind to the realities of my own habits and behaviors.

Having such an intense focus on completing tasks often causes me to become fixated on doing things the right way all the time no matter what the cost or the number of casualties. Autism means that I can be very linear and extremely black and white. I'm often such a rule follower that I struggle being flexible and graceful, and usually the person who suffers the most from my lack of grace is me.

I am my own worst critic and my own worst enemy. While intense focus and fixation on completing tasks is a benefit of my autism, the insistent need to do everything right is not one of my best qualities. After my diagnosis, I observed how this issue contributes to a myriad of complications for me. Sometimes I move very slowly when processing a decision or making a critical choice because I don't have the grace for getting things wrong. Other times, I can be secretly critical of other people's ideas and opinions because, after all, I have processed it for so long that I can't possibly be wrong about my choice. Either way, I have observed the lack of grace in how I handle myself in these situations and have learned to focus on a key principle in trying to find the correct balance. I have learned to focus on doing the right things instead of focusing on doing everything right. After all, being perfect is worth less than being human.

## Spiritual Growth Instead of Religious Activity

Being autistic and being a pastor sometimes defines my behavior in ways that I am not always completely aware of. Sometimes the combination of wanting to be a good example to my congregation and my most natural instinct to stick to rules and rituals makes me a prime candidate for becoming extremely religious. Being religious in and of itself is not a bad thing. However, I have the habit of assuming my discipline and routine makes me more spiritual than others.

I work long hours, read lots of books, and study the Bible with great regularity and focus, but it's part of who I am and not just what I do for a living. If I'm not careful, it can totally escape me that biblical history is my primary interest, and it would be even if I weren't a pastor. My love for history is expressed in my passion for the history of the Christian church, and while it has definitely made me a better pastor, it doesn't necessarily make me a better person. If not careful, I tend to have extremely unhealthy expectations of myself and others as it relates to engaging in practices that may or may not actually contribute to my spiritual health. I may not always verbalize it, but I do sometimes expect people to be just as interested in first-century Christian history as I am. There is that side of me that expects people to love it the way I love it, and if they do not, it is easy for me to assume they are not committed to spiritual growth the way I am.

Nothing can be further from the truth. My passion for all things biblical is more likely the result of my personality than my piety, and while it contributes to my spiritual growth, it doesn't guarantee it. In fact, my rules, rituals, and routines can become just another religious routine that serves only to make me feel spiritually superior to others. This isn't helpful in leading a church, and it is especially unhelpful in my own personal pursuit of spiritual growth.

Because of this sobering discovery about my propensity to be overtly self-righteous, I have adopted a strategy to focus on spiritual health rather than religious activity. Lack of growth is sometimes an indication of over-commitment and not a lack of commitment. Learning to embrace my humanity requires me to continually challenge my need to overextend myself. Like many people, I want to be the better at what I do, and I want to be successful at all that I attempt, but the issue is cost and not commitment.

## Eliminating Time Wasters

Time is the only nonrenewable resource we have. Time does not stop for anyone, so time is a resource I've learned to appreciate and respect more since I learned about my diagnosis. The most effective way to practice good time management is for me to identify time wasters, and the most effective way for me to make those decisions is to identify how much sensory input I can manage on a daily and weekly basis. Sensory processing issues are something many people on the autism spectrum live with. I like to tell people that my life is lived in 1080p high definition, while most non-spectrum people are on 480p, and that's being pretty generous. My brain doesn't normally succeed at filtering out the flood of senses that a typical brain does, so my brain is constantly in overdrive as it tries to filter through every sound, sight, smell, smell, and sometimes taste.

What this means is that I can't use traditional methods for managing my time. Most people don't realize how seamless their sensory integration is on a normal day, so it's really difficult to understand how taking time off during the day and week to "play" is a good use of time management. What could be a waste of time for most people is, for me, valuable time spent reducing the amount of wear and tear on my brain.

When I injured my Achilles tendon in 2012, I was restricted to desk duty only, but for me, that meant spending the majority of my time at home. At the time, I had a full load of doctoral classes and was nearing the end of the semester. I had tons of work due just two weeks after my surgery. Pain management was still a moving target, so I was taking pain medication that disrupted my usually intense focus on my interests. To make the deadlines, I had to become hyper-focused, and it would come at an extreme price.

For days on end, I was locked indoors, which is not so bad, but I read several books in their entirety and spent hours writing sizable papers. My brain was exhausted—in a good way—but if you can imagine the exhaustion of being locked indoors and reading and writing for two weeks straight, then picture my brain working ten times as hard on just processing incoming images, smells, and sounds on a daily basis. If you think of your brain as tires on a vehicle, then you'd see that too much activity can wear down the tire tread, making it difficult to navigate your vehicle without an increased risk of it malfunctioning and causing harm to you or others. When I talk about eliminating time wasters, my goal is to successfully manage the number of miles I put on my "tires" so that I don't wear out the tread too soon. To others, eliminating time wasters will almost always look like I am actually wasting time.

To prevent further damage, rest is necessary. I learned this important lesson the hard way the same summer I injured my leg. Many autistic people have reported trouble sleeping. I experience this primarily because my brain has been going one hundred miles an hour all day trying to process ridiculous amounts of input. On occasion, an hour playing video games helps me to slow my brain down because it takes my mind off of the day. What is normally considered a waste of time actually becomes the best use of my time when I am trying to reduce the wear and tear on my "tires."

I used to feel extremely guilty about this, but after my diagnosis, I understand it more clearly. "Wasting" time for me was actually a way to avoid wasted time later. Treadless tires have no traction, and that leads to spinning wheels. Without my regularly scheduled breaks from the real world, my brain becomes so worn that I end up spinning my wheels at every task I attempt to complete, and it usually just ends up in a downward spiral into one of two outcomes—a meltdown or a shutdown. From the outside looking in, my choice of a hobby would classify me as a time waster, but you don't earn a doctorate degree while pastoring a church full-time along with being a husband and father if you don't manage your time effectively. Eliminating time wasting includes scheduling time to rest so that we don't spin our wheels later and use up unnecessary energy.

## Monitoring My Margin

Restoring a sense of humanity is a pretty grand idealistic notion, and while it can be done, it cannot be maintained without a system for monitoring the process and the progress. This would be a great challenge for anyone, but being autistic requires me to develop a system for monitoring my limits that may or may not include conventional thinking. In many ways, my system for monitoring margin must counteract what many times makes me the most comfortable—isolation.

There's a story in the Bible that often helps me to understand when my need for isolation and seclusion is manipulating my margin. It is extremely difficult for me to manage because, after all, I am prewired to love alone time, but in order to be the best I can be,

I have to be willing to admit when my alone time begins to jeopardize what's really important in life.

Luke records that one day Jesus went to visit his good friends Mary and Martha. If you follow their relationship status, then you would know that Mary, Martha, and Lazarus were siblings that were very close to Jesus, and whenever he was in town, he would stay with them. Like any person blessed with the gift of hospitality, Martha wanted to make sure that Jesus had a good visit. As it turned out, Martha was busy preparing the home and the meal, but when Jesus actually showed up, her sister did nothing to help her serve their guest.

Martha, who was rightfully annoyed with her sister, turned some of her anger toward Jesus because it seemed as though he was completely oblivious to the fact that Mary was being a slacker. "Lord, doesn't it seem unfair to you that my sister just sits here while I do all the work? Tell her to come and help me." But the Lord said to her, "My dear Martha, you are worried and upset over all these details! There is only one thing worth being concerned about. Mary has discovered it, and it will not be taken away from her."[49]

What I learned from this story is that I have a bit of a Martha complex. Granted, I don't see myself as being the anxious host who is compelled to make every social event perfect, but I do see myself becoming so easily focused on what I am doing and my need to complete what I am doing that I have a tendency to totally miss the moment. Until I was diagnosed, I never really considered how much of a struggle I had in being able to live in the moment, to be fully present, and to be engaged with those near to me.

Mary was busy preparing a meal, and my wife tells me that when we are entertaining or involved in a social setting, my most natural response is to take on a task so as not to be overwhelmed by the moment. Most often this means I become laser-focused on

---

[49]Luke 10:40-42 NLT.

monitoring our children, but in doing so, I often miss the moment of the occasion for which we gathered. Mary's problem is similar to mine in that she totally missed the moment to interact with a very important guest, and in doing so may have missed the opportunity to make a new memory that may very well have changed the course of her life.

Maximizing the moment and making new memories is one of the biggest parts of being human. The ability to connect with people and take time to be present with them in ways that contribute to the creation of your own narrative is what makes human socialization so powerful, and being autistic can often make it difficult to choose the moment. So my challenge to myself is one that may also be a challenge for you to consider. Always choose what is irreplaceable.

By now you must have certainly realized that what makes life work for me is almost the opposite of how most things work for others. Making sure that I stay healthy by creating boundaries means I have to also concede that my boundaries don't draw lines that divide me from experiencing the things in my life that are absolutely irreplaceable. I love to be alone. I love my moments of isolation. I very rarely have any desire to leave the house, but as much as I love those parts of my personality, I love my family more.

My wife and my children and many other people that love and support me are irreplaceable. When Jesus responds to Martha's main issue, he points out to her that Mary has discovered what's important in life, and not even he is willing to come between her and "it." If you ask me, that's a pretty powerful statement. Jesus refuses to use his influence and power to disturb the moment because the moment set aside to connect with Mary, and for Mary to connect with him, is something that can't be replaced.

My irreplaceable "it" is my family, and no matter how much I would love to lean into my natural desire to be alone most of the time, ultimately it is not healthy for me because it jeopardizes my relationship with them. That means that I often have to make a choice. When I become aware of how much time I have spent away from my kids, I have to choose to go out with them into the world, into sensory overload, into varying degrees of social anxiety and fatigue because they are irreplaceable, and I choose them over isolation. When I become aware that I have spent most of my time at home upstairs reading, watching television, or playing video games, I realize I must choose to spend time with my wife because she is irreplaceable.

The reality is that not choosing what is irreplaceable is actually irresponsible. Building so many barriers and boundaries into my life that it makes it hard to choose the people that I am doing life with is irresponsible, and when I begin to sense that happening, I know that I am not living my best and most inspired life because I am letting the moments and the memories slip right through my fingertips.

Martha's story has helped me to develop a simple measurement tool to help me avoid missing the moment, and you may find these warning signs helpful for you, too.

## 1. Busyness

This level always begins with an inflated sense of importance. Martha seemed to think that her tasks were the *only* necessity in the moment. I admit that being autistic comes with a hyper-focus that drives me to believe that whatever I am doing is the only thing that is important in the moment, but the reality is that it leads to an inflated sense of importance. The dangerous trap to this type of thinking is that you eventually develop the concept that everything revolves around you and that nothing can be done or done correctly unless you do it. I have been in this place multiple times and still struggle with it on a weekly basis. Like Martha, I can sense this when I have multiple tasks I fail to complete because I have somehow determined I am more important than I am. The end result is almost always that nothing really gets accomplished on my watch.

At this stage, I find that I don't relate well to myself. I get easily frustrated with myself and, like Martha, I become a martyr for my own cause, and it's usually without a cause.

## 2. Blaming

It is always easier to blame than it is to change. When I reach this stage, I usually become agitated like Martha and blame others for what I haven't been able to complete. If I am not able to finish my game or finish my book, I begin to point the finger at everyone else. The problem with this stage is that I don't relate well to myself or to others. No one wants to be around me, so I do eventually get the alone time I need, but the price is far too great to pay for the type of isolation I end up purchasing. When I've reached this level, I know I have chosen incorrectly. I chose something that I could replace over something truly irreplaceable. This is where moments are missed, and memories are forfeited.

## 3. Belief System

By the time I reach this stage of the game, I have drawn lines around all of my relationships, including God. Like Martha, I begin to put God in the center of my dissatisfaction with self and others, assuming that God had the intention of interrupting my quest for quiet. The most important thing to remember about this stage is that it is the beginning stage of no longer living for the ideal. God represents all that is ideal, and that generates a sense of hope and passion for life beyond present difficulties. When I find myself no longer hopeful or no longer trying to reach for my dreams, I know I have gone way beyond my boundaries by compromising the most important relationships in my life. When I am here, I have not only chosen what is replaceable, I have altogether lost a sense of what should be irreplaceable.

Ultimately, living life on the spectrum presents some challenges because of the many roles I play that frequently require me to choose what I want most out of life even in the face of what makes me the most comfortable. While the result of my decisions often appears to come easily, it is by no means an easy task to live in two worlds that you must navigate in order to be successful. Although I had to embrace the reality that being autistic comes with challenges, I would finally learn that the road to discovering my true self and my true strength was paved with my weakness.

# CHAPTER 8
# I AM STRONG

March 8, 2015 was a day that changed my life forever. The date is so significant that I treat it like a birthday or a wedding anniversary. It was one of those moments that are so important that you want to make it a "life event" on your Facebook page. It was an important day for me because it was the day I decided to take a courageous step by standing on the stage of my church auditorium and telling my entire congregation I was autistic.

My diagnosis had officially been given in December of 2014, just one year after being named the pastor of New Community Church. I love my church, but I was initially uncertain as to whether they could handle hearing that they had just been appointed an autistic pastor. Although the elders and the staff knew about my diagnosis, I was confident that the majority of the church wouldn't understand.

Autism is a broad spectrum, and while most people in the autism community are well-educated, many who are not directly impacted by autism are unaware of what it really is. Disabilities and mental health make people uneasy. Although we have taken steps in our society to support those with physical disabilities, we still have a lot of work to do when it comes to recognizing and supporting persons with invisible disabilities. In no place is this more true than in the faith community.

As a pastor, I have observed that most churches and faith communities don't handle disabilities and mental health very well. Perhaps this is because it feels awkward to talk about disabilities inside the church walls. Christianity has a long history of misunderstanding and misinterpreting disabilities, and you can even find occasions in the Bible where physical and mental disabilities were associated with sin or a lack of faith. I understood this all too well, so making the decision to communicate my autism diagnosis to my church was not an easy one. In fact, I was afraid that doing so would cost me everything.

I can imagine this was Paul's dilemma when he was considering talking about his "thorn." Opening up about something so deeply personal can be scary, and I imagine it wasn't as easy a decision for Paul as we so often romanticize it to be. I knew that if I was going to make the right decision about talking about my own self-discovery, it would be because I was confident that I could take a page from Paul's playbook and make it work for me the way it seemed to have worked for him. So what was the reason Paul was willing to bare himself to the world? He tells us in his confession just why he did it. When I read his words, it was as though the words leaped off the page and into my heart. It convinced me that sharing my autism diagnosis with the world was not only a good idea, it was necessary. "So now I am glad to boast about my weaknesses, *so that* the power of Christ can work through me." [50]

Perhaps Paul realized that strength, real strength, is not found in our ability to successfully hide behind our need to present ourselves as stronger than we really are. In exposing his thorn, Paul points to the most important part of being the best you that you were created to be. When he points out his weakness, he gains an overwhelming sense of what truly makes a person strong. Our true strength comes from our creator. I found myself at a crossroads, needing something greater than myself to sustain me for this world. In many ways, getting my diagnosis was a full circle moment that led me back to the very values that shaped my life from the beginning. Being diagnosed with autism spectrum disorder would require me to once again learn how to give my life to something bigger than myself, except this time I would gain strength.

---

[50]2 Corinthians 12:9.

# Faith

For as long as I can remember, I have been an eternal optimist. I am without a doubt a glass half full kind of guy, and while my approach to life has at times frustrated the people around me, it has been my greatest asset in living with autism. I can't always claim that I have been a person of great faith in God, but I can say that I have almost always been a person who believed beyond what I could see in front of me.

As a child, I was extremely stubborn. I was the most stubborn when I met opposition that told me I could not be or do something I had already set my mind on. No matter how hard I tried, when I got an idea in my head and mustered up the courage to act on it, I could not let it go. It was like an obsession, but not always with being first or even being the best—it was an obsession with finishing.

Looking back, I suppose this deeply engrained trait was as much a part of my autism spectrum disorder as it was my character and personality. I like to finish things. I become extremely frustrated and angry when I am unable to focus all of my attention and energy on what I am trying to accomplish. Whether it's reading, writing, playing video games, or finishing a thought when I am conversing with someone, I loathe the thought of leaving something unfinished.

In the past, this did not serve me nearly as well as it does today. When you're a child living with undiagnosed autism, your extreme rigidity is often considered insubordination. Who hasn't become upset with a child who can never seem to step away from what they are engaged in when asked to shift gears to something new? My older sister recalls that I was extremely difficult as a child, but with no real understanding of what I was facing, I was just disciplined.

I still struggle with this issue as an adult, although "meltdowns" are far less frequent (yes, I still have them from time to time) and look quite differently as an adult. As I have grown older and started my own family, I find this to be a continual challenge because managing three children, a marriage, and a ministerial career forces me to operate quite differently than if I were left alone to totally do what I want. If it were not for my duties as a father, I would probably not leave the house because I would be wrapped up in something that I couldn't pull myself away from.

I have learned this can be a weakness when I'm left to my own devices. On the other hand, it can become a great strength when placed in the hands of someone far greater than me. My natural need to focus serves as the engine for my life of faith, and my faith, in turn, helps me to live life on the autism spectrum in ways that showcase the strength and power of God.

Faith requires focus. Giving yourself to something larger than yourself is never a matter of convenience; it is a matter of commitment and concentration. For what it's worth, faith is not a feeling, it is a decision, and it is a decision that demands a response, especially when faced with obstacles. People often marvel at how well I have done considering I have lived the majority of my life as an autistic person who has never been diagnosed. Although I now see a therapist once a month to help me process things, I've never had a professional diagnosis or any professional help, so the most stabilizing force in my life that has helped guide me through my autistic life is faith.

There is probably no other story in the Bible that illustrates the way that faith has influenced my life than the story of Peter walking on the water. My very first sermon as a young minister was this exact story. At the time, I had no idea that I was autistic, but I did know I couldn't continue to ignore what I felt to be God calling me to become a pastor. I had no idea I was autistic, but I did know I was awkward, so awkward that I didn't even talk about my "calling" to anyone for over a year because, quite frankly, there was no one to whom I was close enough and felt I could trust that story to. When I finally did get up the courage to defy every fiber in my being that was trying to convince me what I could *never* do, it was this story that changed my perspective in life.

Immediately after this, Jesus insisted that his disciples get back into the boat and cross to the other side of the lake, while he sent the people home. After sending them home, he went up into the hills by himself to pray. Night fell while he was there alone. Meanwhile, the disciples were in trouble far away from land, for a strong wind had risen, and they were fighting heavy waves. About three o'clock in the morning, Jesus came toward them, walking on the water. When the disciples saw him walking on the water, they were terrified. In their fear, they cried out, "It's a ghost!" But Jesus spoke to them at once. "Don't be afraid," he said. "Take courage. I am here!" Then Peter called to him, "Lord, if it's really you, tell me to come to you, walking on the water." "Yes, come," Jesus said. So Peter went over the side of the boat and walked on the water toward Jesus. But when he *saw* the strong wind and the waves, he was terrified and began to sink. "Save me, Lord!" he shouted. Jesus immediately reached out and grabbed him. "You have so little faith," Jesus said. "Why did you doubt me?"[51]

Peter walking on the water with Jesus is one of the most famous stories in the entire Bible. Even those who don't necessarily believe the stories of the Bible have heard about this story, and it has become a type of colloquialism regarding the role of faith. Walking on water is a universal phrase synonymous with taking a risk of faith, but it wasn't the act of walking on the water that intrigued me about this story. It was the cause of Peter's downfall that captured my attention.

Matthew says that Peter's biggest mistake in using his faith to walk on water was that he lost focus because he started to pay attention to the wind. This statement has always perplexed and

---

[51]Matthew 14:22-31 NLT.

intrigued me at the same time, "But when he *saw* the strong wind and the waves, he was terrified and began to sink."[52] Matthew states that Peter *saw* the wind. My question has always been, "How do you *see* wind?" The reality is that wind can't be seen, but the evidence that the wind is blowing can be seen, and that's what ultimately caused Peter to sink—he lost focus on Jesus because he began to look for evidence that supported why he shouldn't be able to walk on the water.

Whenever you focus on the reasons why something cannot or should not work, you will find exactly what you're looking for. Whenever you need a reason not to try, you will find one. Whenever you search for a reason to doubt yourself and doubt God, you can find one every single time. The Bible is full of people who momentarily lost their faith because they lost their focus on what God could do with them, and instead turned their focus to all of the reasons why they could not succeed. Gideon was a nervous wreck, David's father didn't believe he could be king of Israel because he didn't look like a king, Moses thought his speech problems disqualified him from succeeding at fulfilling God's call for him to lead, and when I found myself diagnosed with autism spectrum disorder at age 36, I added myself to the long list of people who believed they were too weird or too weak to accomplish anything significant with their life, even if God had called them to do it.

Looking for *"wind"* will always cause us to forfeit our future. Looking for *"wind"* will always cause us to fall short of our greatest potential. Looking for *"wind"* when trying to walk on water never works, and it always makes our faith journey worse. Matthew says that Peter was "terrified" when he saw the wind and the waves because the realization that God is calling you to do something that should not be done, based on your ability, is actually terrifying. There is nothing scarier than knowing that you are standing only on faith and not your ability or functionality. When Jesus finally

---

[52]Matthew 14:30 NLT.

rescues a sinking Peter, his question is about Peter's faith in him and not his faith in himself.

When Paul reveals his struggle with his "thorn," he is, in essence, revealing that he had a struggle with his ability to function as a result of this issue. It is though he finally comes to a realization that he is human, but it is his admission that gives him access to his greatest asset, God's strength. What he could or could not do was no longer as relevant as what God could do. After three prolonged seasons of praying that God would remove his thorn, he stopped looking at the wind and turned his focus on God's ability to work through his thorn and produce something extraordinary despite it.

## Wind Watching

Faith requires focus, but one of the most difficult things to do is to understand when you have lost focus. If there is anything I understand well as a result of my autism spectrum disorder, it is having an intense focus on something. My problem is normally the inverse, which means I can have difficulty detaching myself from things that I am intensely focused on so that I can engage in the world around me socially. This is helpful for me, though, because I am able to identify how and when I am focusing on the wrong things, especially when it relates to things that distract me from exercising my faith.

## Pessimism

I am naturally an extremely optimistic person. Sometimes I believe my nature is to go through life with a childlike naivety about many situations. I have the ability to see the best in almost every situation, and this quality has actually served me well and helped me overcome a number of challenges related to my autism. Having a positive outlook on life helps with the ability to recognize solutions to problems and opportunities in obstacles. Now, I realize that everyone is not as naïve as I am. Sometimes life really does look bleak, and the circumstances we face can feel extremely overwhelming, but no matter what your personality is, when it comes to exercising faith, pessimism is almost always a sign that you've been watching the wind.

Peter's story points to how pessimism proves that our focus has shifted to the wrong place. Matthew says that while Peter was walking toward Jesus, he began to look at the strong wind and waves. What's interesting about this description of Peter's distraction is that his eyes become focused on something that can't really be seen at all. When the wind blows, we see trees moving, people's hair blowing, leaves taking flight. We can even see waves in the ocean. The wind, however, cannot actually be seen. What we see is the evidence that the wind is blowing. On the contrary, wind can be felt. We can feel it blowing even though we can't see it, but oftentimes what we feel causes us to search for evidence that validates our feelings.

My point is simply that Peter, like many of us, lost focus because he was looking for evidence to support the feeling that what he was called to do wasn't going to work out after all. In the moments where I lose focus on what is really important, I lose faith in my calling, my purpose, and ultimately my relationship with Jesus. We all look for reasons why something can't work. We all tend to get that nagging feeling that maybe we just can't be more than the statistics say we can be. I will admit that for a few months following my autism diagnosis, I began to feel as though I shouldn't be as accomplished as I am. I felt confused about my identity. I felt confused about my diagnosis. I honestly began to think that either I was not really autistic, or that I was a fraud and everything I was able to do that defied stereotypes about autistic people was a lie or an accident.

The truth is our feelings can often cause us to lose focus because we begin to look for evidence that validates our self-pity. When Peter stepped out of that boat, he was doing so with complete confidence that he could accomplish what he had been called by Jesus to do despite circumstances that suggested he would experience failure rather than success. Wind watching is driven by pessimistic feelings, feelings that look for evidence to support the negative frame of thought. The problem with being driven by feelings is that faith is not a feeling; faith is a decision. If we are ever going to learn to stop watching the wind and start walking on water, we have to make the decision to ignore the reasons why it's not supposed to work and determine that we will focus on what we are called to do and where we are called to go.

## Perfectionism

Most people who spend their time and energy focusing on the wind and waves tend to be perfectionists. If you're anything like me, then you have probably found a way to cleverly disguise addressing this issue. My preferred term is excellence. I enjoy stating that I try to do everything with "excellence," and while there is something to be said about wanting to do the best job possible, perfectionism is a crippling force that robs us of the right type of focus.

The problem with most perfectionists is that we lose sight of the purpose of what we are trying to accomplish and instead focus on perfecting the process. The result is that we often miss the moment in the story when we actually experience, even if temporarily, the success of having had enough faith to step out of the boat and venture out into the waves that threaten to drown our dreams.

It's not uncommon to lose focus on the purpose, and in doing so, it is not uncommon to lose sight of the final product either. I can usually tell when I have lost focus because I fail to realize that success may be right in front of my eyes or right beneath my nose, but I can't appreciate it because the process wasn't perfect enough for me. One of the most interesting parts of Peter's story is that we perfectionists miss something critical to the purpose and the final product of his experience and, subsequently, our experience of faith as well. Peter walked on the water, but what we often neglect to observe is the return trip to the boat. Now Matthew states that Jesus and Peter returned to the boat together after Peter was rescued from drowning by Jesus. Matthew doesn't say this explicitly, but Jesus and Peter got back into the boat together, which suggests that perhaps they walked back to the boat together after Jesus rescued Peter.

The reason it's difficult to observe that part of the story is because when you are a perfectionist, you can't focus on the really important parts of the story. When you are focused on a perfect process, it's very easy to miss the purpose and the final product. Peter did walk on water. He did accomplish what he had set out to do when he stepped out of that boat. His journey wasn't perfect. He lost focus momentarily. He was even reprimanded by Jesus for the size of his faith, but in the end, Matthew says they got back into the boat *together.*

Faith requires focus, but faith isn't always pretty. Sometimes we sink when walking on water. Sometimes the process is difficult, and the reality is it is never perfect. That's the beauty of faith—it doesn't require perfection. If it did, then it would be almost worthless to us. Peter's story shows us that faith requires a focus on how perfect Jesus is, not how perfect our faith is. Being a perfectionist is a surefire way to put an enormous amount of energy into believing that the process is the most important part of faith. Here's my advice—don't miss the forest for the trees. Don't become so concerned with praying the perfect prayer or perfectly memorizing scripture or your perfectly designed plan to execute your faith. Focus your energy on what is most important. God is the author and finisher of our faith. He is perfect even though we are not. How we get there isn't as important as the fact that we *can* get there.

## Panic

One of the most distinguishable identifiers of a loss of focus is the sudden onset of panic. This is difficult to discern because the type of panic of which I speak is not related to a neurological disorder. I have many friends who suffer from anxiety disorder, and as an autistic person, I have had my fair share of anxiety attacks. I understand all too well the feeling of being overwhelmed with the sudden onset of a panic attack. Anxiety disorder can be a very debilitating mental disorder, and because of my experience with it,

I am not attempting to make light of such a complex invisible disability.

The type of panic I am referring to has its roots in the deepest parts of the core of our personality. One of the things I am continually challenged to examine is the depths of my personality. Personality is a God-given design, and it actually communicates a wealth of information that helps unlock God's intention for our life here on earth. Discovering that I am on the autism spectrum has actually ignited a passion in me to further explore all of who God created me to be. In many ways, I believe human beings are analogous to an iceberg. Much of who we really are lies deep beneath the surface of what the world can see. The problem is most of us have become extremely comfortable living on the surface of who God created us to be instead of exploring the depths of divine design.

I am autistic, and autism shapes much of who I am and how I live; however, I also have a personality that is equally unique. I have personal talents, tastes, and desires that are given to me as a part of my design. On top of that, as a Christian, I have been assigned spiritual gifts, given by the Holy Spirit to be used to serve God and others. That's a pretty complex system to understand, and it is even more complicated when we attempt to override it with programming not designed to be compatible with our internal operating system.

What this means is that the type of panic I am referring to is the result of a sudden abandoning of our divinely designed personality and passions. Peter is a pretty passionate individual. In fact, of all the disciples in the boat, he was the only one who had the courage to even attempt to walk on the water. If you know anything about Peter, you know he was a strong personality type. He was energetic and charismatic. Peter was a leader, and it is evident in this story because he was willing to try anything, even if the conditions didn't indicate a very high probability of success. Now, Peter wasn't perfect. He often ended up putting his foot in his mouth. He was extremely reactionary and often didn't give much thought to how he responded to issues. For the most part, though, he was an extremely passionate and faithful guy. In this incident, however, we see a sudden shift from a passionate risk taker to a panicking personality just trying to keep his head above water.

Peter was the one who asked Jesus to walk on the water. Peter was the one who connected his need to know Jesus to an act of complete faith and trust in who Jesus was. Peter was the one who wanted to be close to Jesus in the storm, even if it meant taking a life-altering risk. Peter was passionate about getting out of the boat, but that's who Peter was. He was not a coward, but the moment that things became overwhelming, he became someone he wasn't. Panic is more than just being afraid; panic is about the abandonment of who you are.

I am normally a rather calm and steady person, and for the most part, it takes a lot of "wind" to distract me from my focus. I recognize that much of this trait has to do with my autism. I can spend hours focusing on a task, a book, a video game, or an idea. This is also true with my day-to-day life. I like my routines, and I remain focused when I am allowed to follow my routine and see life through the intensely focused lens of completing my next task. It's because I know this about myself that I can also identify when I am in panic mode.

Like Peter, and probably like you, I have things I want to accomplish, and usually the external factors don't influence my decision to at least try to step out of my proverbial boat. The danger comes not with the wind and the waves but in the way I begin to lose so much focus that I begin acting out of character.

Peter panicked when he began to sink, and as a result, his passion and energy was focused on trying to survive. That's what panic does to you—it takes the best parts of you and redirects that energy into living a life of mere survival. Peter's problem is our problem. We waste the precious energy that is a part of our personality in trying to secure our own survival, when Jesus has already assured us that our eternal security is anchored in who he is.

When we panic and forget who he is, we forget who we are, and when we forget who we are, we settle for just trying to keep our heads above water.

The reality of faith is the responsibility to learn how to focus on the right things. Pessimism, perfectionism, and panic are all just signs that at some point on the faith journey, we have lost focus on what really matters. Being diagnosed with autism as an adult challenged my faith in ways I had never experienced before. The greatest challenge in life is to discover how much we lack, how weak we are, so that we can appreciate how God's strength is found in our weakness.

## From Weak to Strong

The journey to strength is a journey to weakness. Hopefully, you have figured that out by now. I am autistic, but that doesn't make me weak, it makes me human, and while you may know someone with autism, may be autistic yourself, or have some other type of disability or "weakness" that you live through, one thing is certain—we are all human.

For years, I lived an unrealistic life, a life that pushed me well beyond my human limitations. Every struggle I had socially or educationally was the result of my lack of strength, or at least that's what I believed. The life I learned to live was one that had no limitations, no boundaries, and even in the midst of obvious struggles, I was characterized as weak, weird, or just plain wrong.

The most troubling part of living this way is that it eventually eats away at your humanity. When we teach our children not to notice their weaknesses, we teach them not to be human. When we *forget* that we are human, we forget that we are *human*. When we dismiss our own humanity, we create a breeding ground for all sorts of heinous acts against humanity. We teach ourselves and our children not to feel. We teach ourselves and our children to do away with our basic human instinct to have compassion and empathy for the weak and oppressed. We teach ourselves and our children to ignore our duty to the world around us. The absence of boundaries breeds a culture that lacks humility, and a lack of humility always results in a lack of humanity.

When I was diagnosed with autism spectrum disorder at age 36, I understood—perhaps for the first time—that I was human. I understood that my years of struggling with certain issues weren't due to a lack of perfection but an abundance of humanity. I learned that I did have some boundaries and some limitations and that I was indeed human. The journey from weakness to strength is one that requires the traveler to accept limitations as well as appreciate progress.

I don't know if there is ever a day that I don't hear one phrase at least once a day. Sometimes I hear it multiple times a day. What's the phrase, you ask? "You look tired." I admit I hear it all the time, and it used to offend me, but now I just respond with one simple answer, "I am tired." Autism is often accompanied by chronic fatigue, mostly due to sensory overload among other issues. I don't just look tired; I am tired. I am tired almost every time you see me. My face looks exhausted, and my eyes are often red. I live with a condition that causes me to be constantly fatigued, but I am not weak. I am strong.

I am strong because living with autism spectrum disorder means that I live life completely unfiltered. The world as I experience it is dramatically different from most people, and it requires me to pour an incredible amount of energy into surviving each day. I used to think I was weak, but in my weakness, I discovered how strong I am.

My life is like living in high definition, all day every day. My sensory processing issues mean that I see, hear, feel, and sometimes smell the world in ways that most people don't. A typical brain probably filters out most of the noise and visual distractions and odd smells and odors, and in many ways, your brain manages all that for you so you don't have to be overwhelmed by it all. It's actually a lot of work, and sometimes it's overwhelming, so I don't just look tired, I *am* tired, but I am not weak. I am strong.

I am strong because I have fought with the passion and tenacity it takes to step out into a world of sensory overload and social anxiety and put on the performance of a lifetime. I'm doing the heavy lifting. I am strong because I choose to engage rather than retreat, and even on the days I just can't step out of my comfort zone, it doesn't make me weak, it makes me strong enough to understand just who God has created me to be.

The journey to strength means taking the time to know who God has created you to be because God's strength is made perfect in the weakness of our human condition.

Since my diagnosis, I have slowly learned to embrace my humanity. When I need to spend some time alone away from the sensory-overloaded world I encounter every day, I remind myself that I am not weak. I am human, and I am God's creation, and when I run into my human limitations, I find God's strength. Perhaps that was Paul's revelation after all. Perhaps that is why it is okay for us to embrace our own humanity and embrace our weaknesses so that we can truly be strong.

Learning to embrace my humanity has actually made me a stronger husband, father, and pastor. My wife and I have three beautiful boys. When I was diagnosed with autism spectrum disorder, I was worried about whether or not I had been a good dad to my children, a good husband to my wife, and a good pastor to my congregation. When I was diagnosed, I honestly struggled with the idea that I may not be strong enough to handle the three most important roles in my life. The journey from weakness to strength means searching for the ways that perceived weakness can be used by God as strengths. I discovered a few ways that perhaps my autism actually served me well in fulfilling my roles as husband, father, and pastor.

Embracing our own humanity gives us the insight and intent to learn to more consistently embrace the humanity of others.

Learning that I am autistic has liberated me from the prison of conformity. It has persuaded me to extend the same grace and love to others who are also human, who make mistakes, and who live with their own limits, and yet are no weaker than I. I know now that they, too, are human. Learning to extend grace to others is a huge part of becoming stronger.

Human weakness is a vast as the autism spectrum itself. Our commonality of weakness is a beautiful mess that takes place inside the boundaries of weakness, and the fact that there are so many differences is what brings hope to humanity. I have discovered that different does not equal deficient, limitations don't equal liability, and boundaries don't have to translate to burdens. My autism is restoring my faith in humanity because I'm learning how to be human. Learning how to hurt, how to seek help, how to heal, and how to hope gives me the ability to hunt for the best in others who are also in desperate need of having their humanity recognized, respected, and celebrated with grace, love, and acceptance.

"So now I am *glad* to boast about my *weaknesses*, so that the power of Christ can work through me. That's why I take pleasure in my weaknesses, and in the insults, hardships, persecutions, and troubles that I suffer for Christ. For when I am weak, then *I am strong.*"[53]

---

[53]2 Corinthians 12:7-10 NLT.

# ACKNOWLEDGMENTS

A former professor, Dr. Robert Michael Franklin, once stated that "Your education does not belong to you, it belongs to the people you serve." Those words of wisdom pierced my soul, and often serve as the source for my developing appreciation for sharing my life with the world.

To my wife, Isabella, I thank you for allowing my to serve you as your husband, best friend, and father to our beautiful children. Your love and support is the fuel that I need to achieve all that God is calling me to be, and all whom God has called me to serve. To my children, thank you for your love and laughter.

To the staff and elders of New Community Church, thank you for you unconditional love and support throughout this process. May God continue to bless our community with the opportunities to reach those far from him as we serve together.

Finally, to the wonderfully diverse community of Christ followers at New Community Church, for your thoughts, prayers and most of all your acceptance, thank you.

80880199R10090